2004
Cor

TEST MATCH
SPECIAL 3

TEST MATCH
SPECIAL 3

Edited by
Peter Baxter

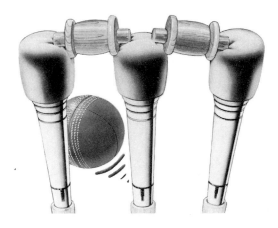

Queen Anne Press

A *Queen Anne Press* Book

© Queen Anne Press 1985
Scoresheets copyright © Bill Frindall

Illustrations by Paul Russell

First published in Great Britain in 1985 by
Queen Anne Press, Macdonald & Co (Publishers) Ltd,
Maxwell House, 74 Worship Street,
London EC2A 2EN

A BPCC plc company

British Library Cataloguing in Publication Data
Test Match Special 3
   1. Test Match Special (Radio program)
   1. Baxter, Peter, 1947–
   791.44'72   GV928.G7
   ISBN 0-356-10775-2

Typeset by J & L Composition Ltd, Filey, North Yorkshire
Printed by R J Acford, Chichester, Sussex.
Bound at The Dorstel Press Ltd, Harlow, Essex.

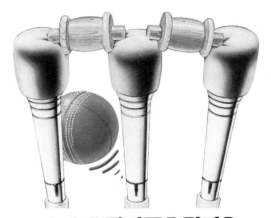

CONTENTS

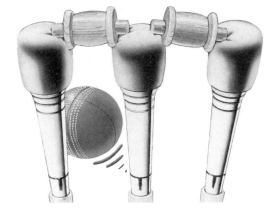

INTRODUCTION

——— Richard Stilgoe ———

They are I suppose, the last people left who really speak English. They get a lot of practice, of course – no other broadcasters have to ad lib for five days at a time. The results have meant that thousands of us during every Test Match switch on our television sets and turn the sound down. We then move the radio to a point where it doesn't squeal too much, and create our own simulcast. We don't do this during Wimbledon, or through the football season. Just for cricket. Because they cheer us up.

Now the chaps in the television commentary box are a perfectly pleasant lot – hair neatly brushed, shiny shoes, nice stripey ties, thousands of runs and wickets between them. But I've seen the hunted look in their eyes. They *know* that everyone listening has the sound turned down. The radio commentary box next door is a different world. It doesn't matter what you look like on the radio, and the TMS cubicle takes full advantage of this. There are never less than 20 people in it – most of them visiting gladiators of the game's past. The commentators sit in a line along the front, looking out of the window. It looks like the bridge of a destroyer which is doing a little rum-running on the side. There is Frindall the navigator with his charts, Captain Johnston in non-regulation co-respondent shoes, First Lieutenant Martin-Jenkins, Lieutenant Commander Blofeld, C.P.O. Mosey and always the visiting native pilot to guide them through the names of the away team. (He is addressed as Sonny, Jammy or, one marvellous year, Prince. That was the year we played the Alsatians.) Behind them sits Admiral Bailey to make sure everything is 'c'rect'. You could film them all, and call it 'In Which we Swerve', or 'The Cruel MCC'.

BBC

The rest of the space in the cubicle is occupied by cakes – the results of Brian Johnston's constant appeals for food over the air. Well, not *appeals* – he just thanks for the last one, and the next sort of arrives. ('While Holding's walking back, may I just say that we really are awfully grateful to Mrs Betty – I think it's Betty, can't quite read your writing, anyway, jolly nice of you – Betty Frampton of Cranbrook for this splendid chocolate cake. It *is* good, isn't it?') and during this, he will have checked which of his colleagues has the fullest mouth, and this will be the man invited to reply.

Not many cricket boxes bear looking inside. Test Match Special's does, containing as it has for years a gang of naughty old schoolboys with a common passion. And gosh, how we needed them in a year when we lost almost every match. Though, admittedly, only on run difference. Let's hope next season is less depressing. Or soon we'll have to listen to the television and watch the radio.

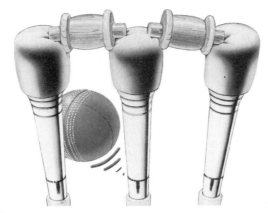

PLAIN TALES OF TMS

TONY LEWIS

On the day I flew to Alderney there were high winds, low mists and rain squalls. I was bent, hurrying across the tarmac when I caught my first sight of John, an outline behind the misty, wet window panes of the small hut which passes for an arrivals-departures reception. I got closer and saw his scowl. Unmistakable: leaning forward, hands on a ledge, supporting the bronchials, just as he had been when I saw him on that day at Lord's when he finished his last Test Match commentary in August 1981.

We shook hands and the Arlott eyebrows raised like a couple of bows suddenly arched and the scowl became a smile like a dark storm lifting. He had his old leather briefcase with him and our mutual BBC friend, David Rayvern Allen, who would produce our endeavours to mark his seventieth birthday with half an hour's reminiscence for radio listeners. The leather briefcase was put up on the counter: out came three glass goblets and a bottle of white Burgundy. It was three o'clock in the afternoon and people were about their business. That knowledge took our reunion way above the commonplace. Unforgettable. He did not look well ... or rather he looked well but did not sound it. The bronchials were indeed playing him up.

Arlott then became guide and chauffeur around the fortress island of Alderney. 'Geoffrey Moorhouse found the old German forts depressing,' said John. They did look bleak.

He drove a little car mainly in second gear. It stopped on a savage, twisted hill. He revved it brutally; stopped, re-started, took a run at it, cursed it, until finally the poor car expired, still in second. I thought, here is a friend so humane and weepingly considerate of humans, flogging this poor small donkey of a car on its final, impossible mission.

A lady from the local shop drove us home in hers.

Home is The Vines, an elegant, handsome house, known before John's purchase as Balmoral. 'Couldn't possibly be caught out having a house with a grand name like that.' I agree. The Vines is perfect. In coloured glass above the front door is a bunch of grapes, and in a large rear garden, walled from the sea winds, are Arlott's own living vines.

Why Alderney? 'The most peaceful place I know. It's cut off. You have to fly. There's no vandalism. I have good memories here.'

Is he still working? 'I'd go mad if I didn't. Couldn't sunbathe or go on cruises. Must write. Great difference between wanting to write and writing for a living, I know, but I just have to.'

Does he follow cricket? 'Yes, but I miss the people more than I miss the game. I miss the radio commentary team, but I don't miss the travel. So much travel and the long roads home: ringing up from a telephone box, perhaps with Clive Taylor when he was alive or John Woodcock, because we lived in the South, and saying to my wife, 'Hello luv. On the way.'

Can he see cricket matters more clearly from a distance? 'No. For instance, I cannot see the Boycott affair any clearer from Alderney than I did from Hampshire. Could see it coming, that's all. He didn't fit. That's the tragedy. He didn't fit, not with cricketers, and, I promise you, cricketers are the nicest people I've known: not more than four bad ones in a lifetime.'

And how does John Arlott live? 'It's seven miles to France. Twelve minutes by plane to Cherbourg. Market day there, the *marché vert*, is superb – Normandy butter, cheeses, it's splendid; and the wine comes across three times a year in shipments from England, and, of course, from my trips to France, Portugal and Spain.'

And next? 'I have reached seventy without disillusionment from the doctors. I've got a chest like a pair of bagpipes full of dust. I get by.'

A fortnight later he wrote a letter to say that he had taken my advice. He had sent his small car on to a new loving owner and had bought himself an automatic.

BRIAN JOHNSTON

How lucky can you be. It was very hot one morning when I left my hotel to go to the Old Trafford Test. I slung my jacket into the back of the car and, in an open-neck shirt, drove off to the ground. It was only when I sat down in front of the microphone that I realised that I had forgotten to bring a tie. It may seem strange but I always wear one when broadcasting and feel quite undressed without. On Thursdays I wear the TMS tie, on Fridays the Cornhill, on Saturdays the Primary Club, on Mondays the Kent Hoppers, and on Tuesdays any one of my many hundreds of cricket club ties.

So when I started to broadcast I explained what had happened and how naked I felt without a tie. Within half an hour a beautiful silk light blue and grey striped tie was delivered to the box. A gentleman with an office near to

Old Trafford had heard my dilemma as he drove to work in his car, and promptly sent me round one of his firm's ties. A nice friendly gesture and I often wear the tie.

Incidentally Vic Lewis – band leader, impresario, cricket fanatic and the USA representative in the ICC has written an illustrated book on cricket ties. He has a collection of nearly 3,000 and he told us about them when he visited our box at Lord's. Actually I was a bit hurt because he called his book simply *Cricket Ties*. When he originally told me he was writing the book I had suggested the title *The Result is a Tie*. But his publishers turned down that idea. I wonder why!

CHRISTOPHER MARTIN-JENKINS

The one and only bore in talking about cricket for a living during a season in England, as you will have read and heard many times before, is the motorway travelling which inevitably goes with it. I am not a great sleeper in strange hotel beds, or, more to the point, in stuffy hotel rooms where the alternatives almost always seem to be between suffocating from excessive heat; catching infection, and/or just one's death of cold, from the air-conditioning system, or – in the rare cases where there are windows which open adequately – being deafened by traffic noises and overcome by petrol fumes. It isn't *really* that bad, but on the whole if I can grab an extra night at home before or after a Test Match I tend to do it, even if it means an early morning dash up the motorway or a late night return.

A few seasons ago I had decided not to travel up the day before a Test Match at Trent Bridge but instead got up just before dawn on the morning of the opening day and dressed myself in the murk of my bedroom, doing my best not to disturb my long-suffering spouse. All went well on the journey. The roads were mercifully free of traffic and the M1 relatively unlittered by those orange cones which seem so often to be put out for decoration or to slow the cars down: one never actually sees any re-building of the road taking place. I stopped *en route* for breakfast and had a shave. One or two people looked me up and down rather quizzically. Every now and then someone does recognise you in this profession, so perhaps I should have been flattered; but there was something different about the way they were looking at me that morning. I checked to see that my hair was not sticking up on end more than usual and that my tie was straight. I am not a very natty dresser but this was the first day of a Test series and I had my best suit on. Perhaps they were just thinking how smart I looked.

I got to Trent Bridge at about ten o'clock, parked the car in Hound Road and walked across the ground in full view of the early spectators, after watching the players in the nets for five minutes or so. I could have sworn that a couple of chaps in Nottinghamshire ties said something and laughed as I passed them after saying good morning. Funny, some of these Nottingham folk.

My colleagues began to gather in the box. The usual pleasantries were exchanged. The match began. All, as Byron might have said, 'went merry as a marriage-bell'. I did my first 20-minute session and then decided I needed to nip down to the Gents to relieve myself. I lined up next to an elderly gentleman. We said good morning, briefly discussed the weather and the start made by England, then proceeded with our business. He looked at *his* feet. I looked at *my* feet. At last, it clicked. My left foot had on it a shoe of brown suede and my right a shoe of black leather!

It was not until shortly before lunch that someone in the box also noticed the result of getting dressed in the dark. I was not allowed to forget it for a long time afterwards.

HENRY BLOFELD

There was a brief moment at the start of June when Test Match Special was suspected of having joined the miners' strike. The cricket season had made a peaceful enough start, apart from one or two West Indian bouncers and, of course, Viv Richards' phenomenal 189 at Old Trafford in the first of the three one-day internationals for the new Texaco Trophy. June 20th then saw the quarter-finals of the Benson and Hedges Cup and my broadcasting duties took me up the M1 to Trent Bridge to watch Nottinghamshire play Lancashire.

I set off early from London and, because the annual jamboree of assorted roadworks on the motorway had hardly begun, I made good time. I kept a weather eye on my speedometer, for a slight indiscretion or excess one Saturday morning the August before (while proceeding towards Bournemouth on the M27 to watch Hampshire play the New Zealanders) had left me a little short of good conduct points.

The miners' strike had been in full swing for some while, but on my cricketing travels I had not come into direct contact with it. The appropriate exit off the M1 for Trent Bridge when coming from London is that which is signposted to Nottingham South. About a couple of miles off the motorway the road goes past a huge power station on the left, whose billowing chimneys have been easily visible for some while.

Blithely, I left the motorway and was just beginning to climb the exit road leading up to the roundabout on top of the bridge, thinking I had done pretty well, when, lo and behold, a large policeman stepped into the road with his hand up. I immediately thought, 'Oh golly, my accelerator pedal has run away with me again,' and I had visions of at least three more points being deducted from the meagre ration I had left. These mental pictures soon panned to visions of myself joining interminable queues at ticket offices at various railway stations round the country when my driving licence had become a part of recent history. It was a particularly nasty moment.

I was far from my usual calm self, therefore, when I pressed the button which operated my car window. By the time the young, fair-haired policeman had bent down to look in the window, I was well launched upon my expansive apology routine and I daresay I had already given him a 'My dear old thing' or two. It was the look on his face which made me stop talking and it was not long before he filled the eerie silence. In somewhat less than convincing tones he asked me if I was on flying picket duty. My relief was so profound that for a moment or two I failed to see the humour in the situation. Then it hit me.

'No, no, no, my dear old thing,' I volleyed back at him, grinning from ear to ear, 'do you think I really look like one?'

My dress was probably a little on the al side of fresco, but even if my clothes did not wholly convince him of my innocence, I dare say my voice may have done. He took a mental step backwards of at least 150 miles and I quickly followed up my question.

'As a matter of fact I'm going to Trent Bridge to commentate on the radio about a Benson and Hedges quarter-final tie between Nottinghamshire and Lancashire.'

He recovered himself with immense speed and through a nervous smile he said, 'On you go, sir.'

At the other exit from the M1 there were a good many police and several vehicles they had stopped which were disgorging potential pickets. Farther on at the entrance to the power station there were two police buses and a squad of officers at the ready. I still don't think I really appreciated the humour of it all until I told the story in the commentary box where it was greeted with most undignified howls of laughter. I still looked upon it as yet another near miss.

BILL FRINDALL

The first of the 1984 Test Matches between England and Clive Lloyd's magnificent West Indies team assumed special importance for me. Ignoring the unofficial series of 1970 which involved a Rest of the World XI, this summer's Edgbaston epic brought up my century of Test Matches for the BBC. Besides an unbroken sequence of 92 Tests in England since I made my debut at Old Trafford in 1966, I had been fortunate enough to score another eight for TMS operations in Australia in 1979–80 and 1982–83.

As I had failed to score a century in over 1,000 attempts dating back to 1949 – my best effort remains 91 not out for Canon Hugh Pickles' Oxford Diocesan Clergy! – I thought that I had better make the most of this one.

Edgbaston has always been a favourite ground. It fully deserves its accolade of 'the best appointed cricket ground in the world' and everyone employed there seems to go out of their way to be friendly and helpful. Income from the Warwick Pool has made it possible for the Warwickshire CCC to make Edgbaston an extremely clean and comfortable place to watch cricket. There is even a garden precinct between the main entrance and the pavilion.

Memories of my early visits there are dominated by the courteousness of the long-serving Secretary, Leslie Deakins, and the Club's Chairman, Cyril Goodway. Leslie devoted his life to Edgbaston. He always found time to chat to visitors to his office and was a copious letter-writer. When Brian Johnston tore the leg of his trousers by colliding with the stone pot of a shrub stationed along the path behind the pavilion, Leslie arranged for repairs and wrote BJ a long letter of apology. Brian wrote thanking him for his kindness. Two days later he received another letter from the Warwickshire Secretary thanking him for his thanks. I think the sequence ended there! Cyril Goodway made 40 first-class appearances for Warwickshire as a wicket-keeper between 1937 and 1947. He was a most generous and genial host to TMS and always appeared at the window of our box just before lunch on each day of a Test to collect our drinks orders. His kindness backfired on him when his visit to our window coincided with Don Mosey's first commentary from that box. Not having met Cyril or been briefed about the drinks procedure, Don told the world that he couldn't describe the next ball because 'some idiot is standing in front of our window smiling at me'!

The 1984 Birmingham Test was launched by an Eve of Match Gala Dinner superbly organised by the West Midlands Region of the Lord's Taverners. Over 2,000 sponsors and guests dined lavishly in a giant marquee at the City End of the ground and were well entertained by speeches from Christopher Martin-Jenkins and others. The editor of the programme-cum-menu had very kindly included a note of thanks to me for providing some statistics on England v West Indies Tests. It began: 'The Edgbaston Test with the West Indies brings up a milestone for Bill Frindall, a century of keeping Test records with the BBC'. I don't mind being thought of as an octogenarian bifocled midget – a sort of aged Ronnie Corbett – but that is ridiculous!

Two telegrams awaited my arrival in the box next day. One was from that versatile actor, Lord's Taverner, and Chairman of the Players' Theatre Music Hall, Johnny Dennis. It read: 'Congratulations on your hundred! May your ink never dry up and you see dots before the eyes for a hundred more'.

The second was from my mother who, despite having no particular interest in cricket, has become a devoted listener to TMS. Her message was addressed to: 'Bill Frindall, BBC Scorer, Chestnut Special, Edgbaston'. She still swears that she dictated 'Test Match Special'. Obviously someone at British Telecom has been listening to us!

PETER BAXTER

The Lord's commentary box during a Test Match is a hive of activity. Often it is difficult to pick your way through the people, bags, discarded lunchboxes, teapots and cake-tins. Four times a year, though, I see it in a very different condition: early in the morning for the draw for the quarter- or semi-finals of one of the cup competitions. Donald Carr, the Secretary of the Test and County Cricket Board, with either of the Assistant Secretaries, Mike Gear or Brian Langley, comes up to the box, draws numbered ping-pong balls out of a red velvet bag and Radio 2's audience hear the result as it happens. A few years ago, though, one of these cup draws – with the best of intentions – was made much more complicated. It was decided that in the Benson and Hedges Cup the winner of each of the four preliminary groups should have a home tie in the quarter-finals. Further, just to throw in an extra headache, the runners-up in each group must not meet the winner of their own group.

These draws were always performed during the Terry Wogan Show and a quarter of an hour beforehand I call at Donald Carr's office in the pavilion ready to take him upstairs. On the morning of the Benson and Hedges quarter-final draw in 1984 I arrived as usual at Donald's office door to find it tight shut and the sound of muttered conversation from within. Behind it I found Donald and Mike Gear rehearsing the technicalities of making the draw to fulfil all the requirements. Two velvet bags were in play – each with four ping-pong balls. The first bag was for the home sides – the group winners; the second for the away counties – the group runners-up. As each home team was drawn, the ball representing their runners-up would have to be quickly removed by Mike before he drew the away team. (Are you with me so far?)

With a certain amount of trepidation we mounted the stairs. We grouped ourselves round the single microphone and waited for Terry Wogan to hand over to me with his usual banter about dodging the guard-dogs to get into Lord's. I made a brief explanation of the complications and then we were away. Donald and Mike got through the first three pairings like a train. Warwickshire would play Surrey, Nottinghamshire would meet Yorkshire and Essex would entertain Lancashire. It was all going well. Then abruptly Donald said: 'No, it won't work!'

I had that alarming feeling (not uncommon to those who work in TMS) that the ceiling was falling in on me.

'It won't work,' repeated Donald. 'The other two are both from the same group.' Sure enough a glance at the list showed that Sussex and Somerset would have to meet having both qualified from Group C. From the studio an ecstatic Wogan burbled with glee. 'Press on, lads!' he cried. 'Try again!'

And we did. The balls all went back in the bags and away we went again. This time it worked, with only one tie staying the same – Essex v Lancashire. But Terry was never to let us forget it. Later draws in the season were greeted with lines like 'Well, Donald Carr obviously liked that draw, he didn't want to do it again!'

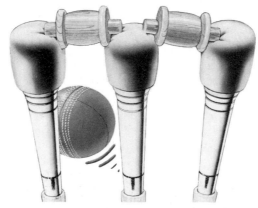

THE 1984 COMMENTATORS
Henry Blofeld

HENRY BLOFELD

Henry – or 'Blowers', as he is universally known in commentary boxes, Press boxes and dressing-rooms around the world – was described in *Test Match Special 2* by Christopher Martin-Jenkins as a deliberate eccentric, which seems to sum up his character. Henry is a *bon viveur* in its fullest sense, believing that life is there to be enjoyed – he lives it at break-neck speed to match his style of commentary. That style has been embraced by the Australians, who apparently regard him as the archetypal 'Pom'. Every year he is to be found sampling the delights of Australian wine and steak 'down under', where he appears to work for about 20 local radio stations. On the first day of the 1982–83 series in Australia I ran into Henry towards the end of play. 'You seem to have been busy,' he said, 'How many reports have you done?' 'My throat's dry,' I replied. 'I've just done my twenty-fifth.' 'Not bad,' said Blowers, 'I've just done my eightieth!'

Henry probably sees more cricket than anyone in the world. A few weeks after the end of every English season, he is jetting off to the Antipodean sun and then, if time permits, he often crams in a couple of Tests in the West Indies before the first ball is bowled at Lord's in April. It all adds to his fund of stories. If you get away with hearing any of them only once in the first few weeks of the season you must be deaf!

Most of all Henry is a good companion, communicating the fun he gets out of life to those around him. This is his assessment of his colleagues in the box.

P.B.

BRIAN JOHNSTON

It would be impossible to imagine a more congenial companion than Brian Johnston with whom to watch a day's cricket, which is surely the principal reason so many people listen to Test Match Special. I can assure you that BJ or 'Johnners' is even better value in the box than he sounds at home. He is a brilliantly professional broadcaster, with more experience than the rest of us put together, and makes up his own rules as he goes along. The trouble comes when others of us try to copy him.

BJ is outrageously funny, splendidly, at times wickedly, unorthodox, enormously kind, an arch practical joker with a genius for communication. I think his secret is his ability to chatter away for ever while making everyone, whether they are in the box with him or listening at home, feel that he is talking especially to them. A life member of the Wicket-keeper's Union (Eton Rambler branch) and pretty brisk to disturb the timbers, too, he has a passionate love of cricket, a prodigious memory for the best (and the worst) music hall jokes, and is a constant maker of puns – mostly too awful for words, but just occasionally superb. I shall never forget a colleague on a tour of the West Indies introducing 'Johnners' to a beautiful friend called Annette. 'My goodness me,' it came, as quick as a flash, 'every time you've told me you were going to go and have "Annette", I thought you meant you were going to play cricket.'

To make a slight play on the title of one of BJ's autobiographies – I don't know whether he or Jim Swanton holds this particular record – 'Johnners' has been and still is the most colossal amount of fun. I can't imagine TMS without him. And if I hear any uninformed knocker say that BJ has ever missed a ball because of chocolate-cake banter, it will be pistols at dawn at the back of the commentary box. BJ is always an early arrival in the box, wearing his brown and white co-respondent shoes, usually beating the first of the chocolate cakes by a short head.

CHRISTOPHER MARTIN-JENKINS

CMJ always introduces a welcome note of calmness – I almost wrote sobriety – into the box. He is a model for any aspiring commentator for he is the coaching manual brought to life. No one tells you better exactly what is going on out in the middle and with a delightfully pleasant flow of description, occasionally interspersed with interesting theories of his own. CMJ is a brilliantly funny mimic, but seldom allows himself the luxury of a performance on air. When he does, people usually think that it is the person he is imitating who is speaking.

The calm, measured tones which make him so easy to listen to are shattered when a batsman is out or there is a near-miss. Then, a shout of such astonished surprise almost gives everyone in the box with him a heart attack, to say nothing of the engineer who is frantically coping with the sound levels and those of you at home who are sent leaping out of your armchairs. From time to time, too, CMJ will innocently suggest to FST that because the human race is nowadays taller than when the game of cricket was invented, the pitch should be lengthened from 22 yards. Rapidly, FST's eyebrows and pipe raise themselves about three and three-quarter inches.

A most competent cricketer, CMJ once made 99 at Lord's for Marlborough against Rugby, before running himself out – if you can beat that. He is a prodigious and diligent writer of books, the most delightful of men, an excellent after-dinner speaker and he ties his ties in the tightest knot I have ever seen. He has also fathered two sons who, if keenness is anything to go by, will certainly play for England.

Invariably one of the last to arrive in the box, he is never there before the producer has pinned the list of odds against the time of his arrival to the wall. It usually reads something like: Five minutes before the start: 7–2. As the umpires are walking out: 5–4. As the batsmen leave the pavilion: evens. In the first over: 5–2. Twenty minutes late: 9–2. In time for opening the bottle of champagne: 100–8.

Chris has recently taken over as the BBC's cricket correspondent – we are in safe hands.

DON MOSEY

'The Alderman' is the wordsmith of the box. While most of us are getting our knickers in a twist with long phrases which seem to trip over each other without ever quite describing, as we would like, the action in front of us, he is able effortlessly to conjure up the precise word or phrase. He goes along at a measured pace and has the ability to stand (or sit) back and look at the game at any particular moment, seeing it in the wider perspective of the contest as a whole.

'The Alderman' has a distinctive delivery which is instantly recognisable and is in sharp contrast to my own galloping burble, for example. He is a pleasure to listen to. His well-chosen phrases always reveal his success in bringing a shrewd Yorkshireman's eye to the game. Never afraid to speak his mind, he will hand out criticism if he thinks it is just and deserved. My own favourite memories of 'the Alderman' come from abroad. In Lahore, in 1977–78 we commentated together on a live riot when, shoulder to shoulder, we sniffed tear-gas. This was the occasion when, with despicable cowardice, the rest of the English media contingent, myself included, fled from the Gaddafi Stadium in our bus without realising that 'the Alderman' was not with us. As was chronicled in some detail in the first *Test Match Special* book, he had to leg it the two miles or so back to the hotel in rough circumstances.

He was a good cricketer himself and has a wide knowledge of the game. He is a hater of all forms of petty bureaucracy and is highly impatient should he come across a lack of professionalism in those with whom he works. His accounts of these verbal battles are often uproariously funny. 'The Alderman' retired as cricket correspondent in October 1984, although happily he will stay with us as a contract man.

He always arrives in plenty of time and likes to have a few jousts at the word game with BJ before the day begins. BJ is the champion, but 'the Alderman' complains that his style of play is monotonous and that he always uses the same words.

TONY LEWIS

There are few more talented and able broadcasters around than 'Arl', whose initials have given him the nickname that I almost feel nature intended for John Arlott. He has a foot in both camps – for half the time he is with us as a commentator and for the remainder he becomes an expert summariser. It must be immensely difficult to do one Test Match as a summariser and the next as a commentator and it is a measure of his skill that 'Arl' slips so easily from one role into the other.

He is always interesting in either capacity for he has a great knowledge of the game and the rare ability to put it across in simple terms which the most humble layman can understand. 'Arl' is unfailingly cheerful – he makes less fuss about hangovers than anyone I know – and is always bringing in the most delightful anecdotes from his own playing days. 'Arl' and I commentated together on the Jubilee Test Match against India in Bombay which will be best remembered for another superhuman performance by Ian Botham and a total eclipse of the sun which caused the rest day to be held on the second day of the match. In 1971–72, 'Arl' captained England in India and Pakistan where he is held in deep affection. It makes life unbelievably easier to travel round the sub-continent alongside him because people invariably come running in droves to assist at those dreadful moments in or outside airports. I am sure no Viceroy ever had things easier than 'Arl'.

An extremely hard worker, 'Arl' is probably the most versatile of all of us in the box, in that cricket is a long way from being his only writing or broadcasting interest. He also won a rugger Blue at Cambridge, was a violinist of considerable talent, a fine singer, has a great appreciation of the arts and is always a splendid companion.

He is never, or almost never, late, although, like me, he has a genius for misreading the times on the commentators' rota, and between us we have turned our producer's hair to an elegant shade of grey.

TONY COZIER

If a poll was taken in all the cricket-playing world, I have little doubt that the nicknameless Tony would come out not only as the best known but also as the best cricket commentator in the world. In the last 15 years or so Tony has done more commentary worldwide than anyone else. He seldom misses a West Indies tour to any part of the world and has at different times joined all

The 1984 TMS team. Back row: Tony Lewis, Henry Blofeld, Ray Illingworth, Christopher Martin-Jenkins, Peter Baxter, Bill Frindall. Front row: Don Mosey, Trevor Bailey, Brian Johnston, Fred Trueman, Tony Cozier.

the domestic commentary teams round the globe. It is a pleasure to see Tony, who is always his same good-humoured self. He has a remarkable ability to adapt his style of commentary to suit the requirements of any particular team he may join.

Tony fits in perfectly with the humorous, throw-it-around, extrovert approach of TMS. In Australia, whether with the ABC radio team or more recently the Channel 9 television commentators, both of whom play it straighter, he is entirely at home; as he is anywhere else. He has a fine sense of humour and commentates without the slightest indication of bias, really appreciating good cricket no matter if it is played by West Indians or by one of their opponents. When I am not commentating on a Test Match I always enjoy listening to Tony, who over the years has been a great advertisement for his country and its cricketers.

When you share a box with him he is always full of the most useful up-to-date information about the West Indian players. Also he is one of the few overseas commentators who has never had any trouble in adjusting to the requirements of broadcasting for the general sports programmes on the BBC, in which timing is all-important and often a whole day's play has to be crammed into, say, 45 seconds.

Tony is an excellent cricketer in his own right – he plays for Wanderers in Barbados – and like all the rest of us in the box, enjoys most of the good things in life. As you would imagine, he is punctual in the extreme, although he dislikes the early-morning, 8.15 stint, and if there were one or two more of us as reliable, our producer's hair might have stayed its original colour – whatever that was.

FRED TRUEMAN

I am sure there can't be anything new left to say about Fred, so I shan't try. I never feel that a day's commentary has begun until I hear Fred's deter-mined, striding steps coming up the stairs, see the pipe in full furnace and hear the resonant, 'Morning, H'. I know it's for real then. Fred has always been a larger-than-life character; in the box as elsewhere. Stories about Fred are legion, mostly untrue and many uncomplimentary, but he takes them all in good part. It says a lot for him that nearly 20 years after he took the last of his 307 Test wickets he is just about as well-known as ever.

Fred has always spoken his mind and has said what he believes to be true. Of course this upsets some people, but if Fred thinks a cricketer has played badly or is not up to it, he will say so. A year or two ago he was voted Radio Sports Personality of the Year, an award which reflects his popularity. I find Fred's views healthy and refreshing – if you ask him a question you get a straight answer, and there is no pussy-footing about. He is always ready, too, to have a laugh with you on the air, and William, his sheepdog, is always a welcome visitor to the box, although he gets a little upset when 'Johnners' makes noises at him.

I know Fred, as a true and devoted Yorkshireman, has been very upset at the problems surrounding the club at the present time, for there is nothing closer to his heart than Yorkshire cricket. Who can blame him if he has occasionally voiced his grievances over the air? He has been accused of being too critical of today's players but Fred is a black-and-white character who will always have strong views, just as surely as there are those who will not always appreciate them. When a puzzled look comes into Fred's face and he says, 'I don't know what's going off out there,' I know he means what he says and if we had played the game to his standard, we wouldn't either.

Fred always clocks in on time. He's early if he comes in the Rolls, but, when it's the BMW, he seems to cut it a bit finer.

TREVOR BAILEY

No player has ever sold himself more dearly or thought much more deeply about the game than 'The Boil', and TMS listeners have the benefit of these thoughts which have come from years of experience with Essex and England. He is very quick to appreciate the significance of what is going on in the middle. Whatever slight adjustment is made in the field, 'The Boil' has the answer. His instincts tell him what a captain, a batsman or a bowler is trying to do at any moment of the game and indeed what they should be trying to do, and, in putting this across to listeners, he is always clear and interesting. He is quick, and almost invariably right, when summing up a new player.

He is very good value to work with and he has a good, if rather dry, sense of humour. He is endlessly ribbed about his own reputation as a defensive batsman which he takes in good part. He laughs at the fact that he lives in a street called The Drive when Defensive Push Lane might have been more to the point. 'The Boil' and I once worked together at Northampton, when Northamptonshire beat Lancashire right at the end of a NatWest semi-final. The other match had ended early and I had to do almost two hours commentary on my own when the NatWest Special programme began at six o'clock. 'The Boil' was a marvellous help and was always ready to nip in with something pertinent so I could swallow a quick drink while a fast bowler was walking back. He was for years, too, our chief source, in the box, of champagne, which was supplied by a firm whose name I forget. After about an hour's play 'The Boil' would disappear and come back a little later clutching a bottle and, grinning broadly, he would say, 'The medicine, the medicine'.

He thinks nothing of driving from Southend to Manchester on the first morning of a Test Match. As a result he arrives a little breathless but almost always in the nick of time. If not, he mutters darkly about contra-flows and traffic jams.

BILL FRINDALL

I doubt if anyone has been more aptly named than 'The Bearded Wonder'. Yes, he has a beard, but it is going to be difficult to do justice to his skill, precision, accuracy and neatness as our scorer and purveyor of information both statistical and biographical. As you can see from his score-sheets in this book, his neatness is phenomenal. He has taken a system which was pioneered by his predecessors and has developed it to its present levels, where it will tell you everything at a glance, except what the twelfth man had for breakfast.

'The Bearded Wonder' has with him a fair number of record books, all inevitably written by himself, and the most comprehensive details about every participant in the game. No sooner has a commentator raised a point than 'The Bearded Wonder' dives into a folder and, before the end of the same over, the details you may have wanted have been put in front of you. It is almost impossible to catch him out and, if at times we seem to rub his nose in it most unfairly when he has made a mistake (there is never more than one a season), it is nothing more than a reflection of the extraordinarily high standard he has set at an extremely difficult job.

We commentators talk for 20 minutes and then have 40 minutes or an hour off. 'The Bearded Wonder' has to maintain his concentration throughout the day and his only breaks come at the lunch and tea intervals. In addition to all that he is doing for us, he is also supplying newspapers with score-boards and statistics, and a constant stream of handmaidens penetrate the box to take sheets of paper from him to be dictated to various copy-takers. While his pen nibs never squeak, I am sure listeners will be familiar with the avuncular snort with which he greets any joke, intentional or otherwise, a mistake or anything foolish the commentator may have said.

He is a passionately keen cricketer who never misses a chance to turn out for the Lord's Taverners and also he has his own touring side, the Malta-maniacs, which he presides over like a benevolent despot.

He is always the first to arrive in the box to set up his papers and stop-watches and things. If anyone should spill anything, tea, coffee or something a little stronger over his sheets ... well, it's advisable not to.

PETER BAXTER

In the preceding pages we have seen our producer's hair go grey and if he reads any further it will probably fall out altogether. 'Backers' has been the boss since 1973 and as far as I know, has not, at the time of writing anyway, bought a gun to shoot either us or himself. He has a thankless task, really, dealing with a bunch of chaps, part-time prima donnas I dare say, some of whom need nannying, some, if not all, organising, some wet-nursing, some disciplining, some feeding and all with thirsts which need regular quenching.

He selects the commentators for each match, arranges the rota, distributes car-park tickets, makes sure the technical operations are OK; produces the coffee before the start, and lunch on the last two days when the sponsors feel we should diet; makes sure one of us is there at 8.15 am to do the piece for the Today programme; records, produces and interviews for the Great

Match which is played during the lunch interval on the first day of each Test Match; arranges for the celebrity who will natter to BJ during Saturday's lunch interval; and is responsible for a million and twenty-one other things besides. And when that's all done, he has to see to it that we produce our chapters for this book on time – on this occasion my offerings were one day late.

On reflection, you might think that the prophet Job had a pretty cushy number. Yet with enormous good humour 'Backers' copes with it all. If you ask him to pour you out a cup of coffee just when the lines have gone down or if you do a more than usually blatant piece of advertising, you may be tempting producerly providence just a fraction. 'Backers' is always there, but never obtrusively so. He is a guiding hand who steers rather than pushes, who suggests rather than exhorts and who has a quiet word in your ear rather than ticks you off. I am sure we take him too much for granted and it is not until you stop and think that you realise how efficiently he operates. He is, too, the most congenial of companions.

Usually, he is second into the box, a short head behind 'the Bearded Wonder'; almost invariably, last out of the box, after tidying up the considerable mess we have all made during the day.

RAY ILLINGWORTH

This was the first year for 'Illy' – we snitched him away from television for a couple of matches and he was an instant success. In recent years there has been no shrewder brain on the field of play and, up in the box, he revealed this, along with a lovely sense of humour which enabled him to fit so quickly and eagerly into the atmosphere. He also has the ability to put his thoughts across in easily digestible form. His comments were always interesting and to the point. He was objective and never destructive and from the moment 'Johnners' turned to him in his first session with us, with a cheery 'Morning Illy,' he played a blinder. Having given up the Yorkshire captaincy only in 1983, 'Illy' was in a marvellous position to talk at first hand about contemporary players and their strengths and weaknesses.

MIKE DENNESS

Mike was another debutant in 1984 and his light Scottish brogue was a welcome addition to the diverse collection of voices that is TMS. He has always been a deep thinker about the game and he was also a great success with his carefully thought-out comments and observations and his unassuming method of delivery. He, too, soon blended easily in with the less than solemn atmosphere of the commentary box. Mike had worked for us before when TMS mounted its own operation on the last tour of Australia in 1982–83. Having only recently finished playing with Essex, Mike also had the advantage of having played with many of the participants on both sides in this series.

He and 'Illy' won't get off so lightly in *Test Match Special 4* when it is written, for by then we will have had more chance to pull their legs, give them red faces and to have a laugh at them. They had better watch out.

GAMINI GOONESENA

Gammy was soon christened 'the phantom tea-planter' by FST because he took a thoroughly cavalier view of the rota for the summarisers during the Sri Lankan Test Match. It was tremendous to have Gammy with us again – he had worked with us in Colombo during Sri Lanka's first Test Match in 1982 – and he was another who wasted no time in picking up the atmosphere of the box. He was a marvellous help, too, in bringing up Sri Lankan players and managers and Board Presidents and Cabinet Ministers for us to talk to. In fact they came so thick and fast that once when Gammy came into the box 'Johnners' who was on air, said, 'Ah, here comes Gammy Goonesena back into the box and I am sure he's got the Sri Lankan Minister for Agriculture and Fisheries with him so we can hear his views on how it's all going.

Gammy was a fine leg-spinner and middle order batsman who once hit a double century for Cambridge in the University Match. At different times he played for Cambridge University, Nottinghamshire, Sri Lanka and New South Wales. Although he has lived lately in Australia, he knew the Sri Lankan players well and made an important contribution to TMS during this match.

He had the last word on Fred about his timing complaints when he discovered that it was Fred who had misread the rota and had most unfairly accused Gammy. Perish the thought, but I think it was 'The Boil' who was late.

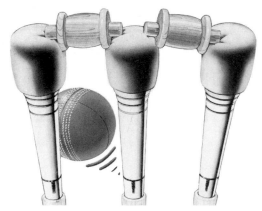

ENGLAND IN
NEW ZEALAND 1983-84
——————Bill Frindall——————

England had already completed the Fijian leg of their winter tour and were comfortably drawing their opening match in New Zealand when I arrived in Auckland in early January. Because of the 12-hour time difference I had managed to hear Don Mosey's reports on the first day's play on the morning I left London, had read an account of the second day during a re-fuelling stop in Perth, and had been driven from the airport on the third afternoon in time to watch the last session of play from the Radio New Zealand commentary box. There was 'the Alderman', resplendent in his shorts and long socks. There too, in his own domain, was Alan Richards. A former Auckland batsman and captain, he has been New Zealand's visiting commentator on all their major tours since 1973. With them, as summariser, was Clive Radley of Middlesex who spends his winters coaching in Auckland. Eden Park must have fond memories for him. In 1978 he batted 649 minutes for 158 runs in a Test there.

Although I spent over ten weeks in New Zealand, that was my only visit to the radio box. TMS were not mounting their own operation or taking ball-by-ball commentary. Don was guest commentator on their domestic network and sent back reports and interviews to the BBC, usually from a separate position. At Eden Park this involved him sitting outside the back door of the box with a phone on his lap. I was out there to score for Television New Zealand who were covering the three Tests and the three one-day internationals. By arranging for my own cricket team, the Maltamaniacs, to tour

both islands before playing a handful of matches in Sydney and Perth on the way home, I had extended my stay by five weeks.

Excess baggage is my major problem on overseas tours. My work demands a small library of books, files, scoring-sheets and associated paraphernalia. Add a cricket coffin full of gear, a typewriter, and clothing, and you have a great deal of luggage. Because of the Maltamaniacs' tour I was able to arrange a contra-deal with British Airways. Their Sports Bureau's budget bore the cost of my excess weight: £828.18. They also made me extremely comfortable in their Club Class and sat me near that marvellous Scottish actor, Fulton Mackay. He was travelling to Bombay for six weeks of filming and declared himself a devotee of Test Match Special. It might have been a very difficult nine-hour flight in close proximity to someone who hated the programme.

Ian Walter had been official scorer to the 1973 New Zealand tour of England and had played for my team. He had invited me to score the 1977–78 series between New Zealand and England but his secretary had posted the letter surface mail and it had reached me a month after the series ended! Now Sports Producer for TVNZ, he wanted me to score, give statistics on air – particularly on the England team, present a pre-play feature called 'Frindall's Figures', and supervise the input for Data General's computerised score-board and career records. The commentary team met for the first time on the eve of the Wellington Test. It was exceptionally strong in batting but lacked a strike bowler: Glenn Turner (Otago, Worcestershire and New Zealand), Khalid 'Billy' Ibadulla (Warwickshire, Tasmania, Otago and Pakistan), John Morrison (Wellington and New Zealand), Warren Stott (Auckland – Rochdale-born, he had been a member of the 1979 Prudential Cup squad), and Peter Williams (staff presenter and commentator).

England arrived in a rainswept Wellington short of match practice and with the outdoor nets awash. Apart from Tavaré, all the batsmen had scored at least one 50 in the matches against Auckland, Central Districts and Northern Districts. Marks, Foster, Botham and Cook were among the wickets. The Basin Reserve pitch was an unknown quantity. After a long, dry spell, some two inches of rain fell a few days before the start of the Test, flooding the unprotected square. Thanks to the strength of Wellington's infamous gales the match began on time after New Zealand had elected to bat on a slow, low surface.

From my position perched on a gantry suspended from the roof of the R. A. Vance Stand directly behind the bowler's arm, it was good to see Botham steaming in with all his old zest. Slimmer after his soccer exertions, he had recovered his ability to swing the ball late and took 5 wickets in an innings for the twenty-first time in 64 Tests. Some 18 innings had passed since he had last achieved this feat. Willis overhauled Fred Trueman's tally of 307

The radio and television boxes up under the roof of the R. A. Vance Stand at Wellington.

wickets to become England's leading wicket-taker and bowled with great accuracy. Dismissed for 219 after eight minutes' play on the second morning, New Zealand could derive satisfaction only from a maiden 50 by the elder Crowe. England were soon in trouble against the bounce and swing of Lance Cairns. Aided by two sensational gully catches by Hadlee and an unlucky played-on by Tavaré, he accounted for the first 5 wickets, the third of which brought up his 100 in Tests. Then he dropped Botham before he had scored and the course of the match changed. By the time Botham and Randall were parted over a day later they had added 232 (Botham 138, Randall 164) and steered England towards a lead of 244.

At stumps on the third day Howarth's side were 93 for 2, still 151 behind and in trouble. The two batsmen capable of shoring up an innings, Wright and Edgar, had both been dismissed. Wright mis-cued a lofted on-drive off Cook only to discover that he had been using a Harrow-size bat! New Zealand were still 79 in arrears when Jeremy Coney joined Martin Crowe. Their maiden Test 100s were the highlights of a magnificent recovery which saved the match. Glenn Turner was particularly impressed with Crowe and remarked that we had seen one of the great batsmen of the future come of age. 'When he learns to place the singles and work the ball around, he'll be even better,' Turner predicted.

He was less impressed with one of my comments. Responding to the producer's request to brighten up the final session of play, I said on air to Glenn: 'Of course it's not generally known that Jeremy's mother invented radio.' 'Really?' he spluttered. 'Yes. Ma Coney!' Nor did he forgive me for taking the photograph of him fast asleep in the commentary box and allowing it to be made into a freeze frame for transmission during later matches.

Wellington, where I was able to spend most of my stay, proved to be my favourite haven in New Zealand. Its scenery is spectacular and I was able to base myself – and the excess baggage – at the home of Ian Walter at Eastbourne on the opposite side of the harbour to the city. Typical of the majority of houses in the area it was timber-built and was perched on a steep hillside. Basin Reserve is the only Test ground in the country that is not a rugby stadium. Our commentary position commanded a fabulous view of the mountainous approaches to the airport.

Christchurch is small, extremely flat, but most picturesque. It was designed by Colonel Light, who also planned Adelaide. The two cities are very similar, almost surrounded by meandering rivers and a greenbelt of parkland. Both are laid out on the grid system. Lancaster Park is a rugby ground without a hint of parkland near it. Our commentary position consisted of the back two rows of one of the stands and was quite the most primitive I have worked in. My small table had to have stilts on its front legs to accommodate the rake in the seating. A freezing wind whistled across the field at us and we were given rugs to wrap round our legs. There had been much discussion about the pitch before the match was played as two recent Shell Trophy matches there had ended on the second day. Only narrowly did the Canterbury Cricket Association decide not to transfer the Test to Napier.

Although the toss was crucial, England probably lost the match when the seventh ball bowled by Willis leapt from just short of a length like a startled rabbit and flew past a stricken Wright and high over Taylor's head to the boundary. After that delivery England's bowlers were convinced that they had only to bowl long-hops to produce unplayable lifters, while their batsmen were confirmed in their pre-match belief that they were contesting a Test Match on a minefield. The dry pitch was a patchwork of saucer-sized mosaics with crumbling edges. They could be rocked by a gentle push. According to umpire Woodward, as Willis brought down his front foot in his delivery stride, he could see the pitch move a few yards ahead. When I returned a month later, large-scale excavations were taking place, and it came as no surprise when the NZ Cricket Council announced that the ground had been removed from the international arena for the 1985 visit from Pakistan.

On this demanding surface Richard Hadlee played one of the great Test innings. He pulled or hooked the bouncers and long-hops and off-drove the half-volleys. His selection, timing and placement were brilliant. But why was Cowans allowed only 4 balls at him (0-0-1-1) while he was blasting 48 runs (11 fours) off 34 balls from Pigott and 24 from 19 of Botham's offerings? The total batting time for the 3 innings was only 11 hours 41 minutes. As we emerged shivering from our blankets we were not sorry about that.

Returning to Auckland for the final Test, England found a very different surface. Once Howarth had gained first use of a traditionally slow, low Eden Park pitch that allowed bowlers no assistance, he was able to bat England out of the match and the rubber. The contest was in its second half by the time he declared, with more than three and a half hours being lost to rain and a variety of bizarre invasions. These included a rampant hound whose exploits were brilliantly described by Don Mosey in a form of rugby commentary. Our video-tape editors linked a recording of it to our television coverage and the result became a collector's item. England's ambitions were reduced to surviving seven sessions. By the time they were dismissed only 57 runs separated the two teams and just 21 minutes of compulsory batting time remained. In stark contrast to Christchurch, an extra week would not have guaranteed a result on Auckland's pitch where batsmen averaged 50.05 runs per dismissal.

A few hours before Bob Willis and his beleaguered troops flew off to Pakistan, my Maltamaniacs arrived from London to begin my second tour of the Land of the Long White Cloud.

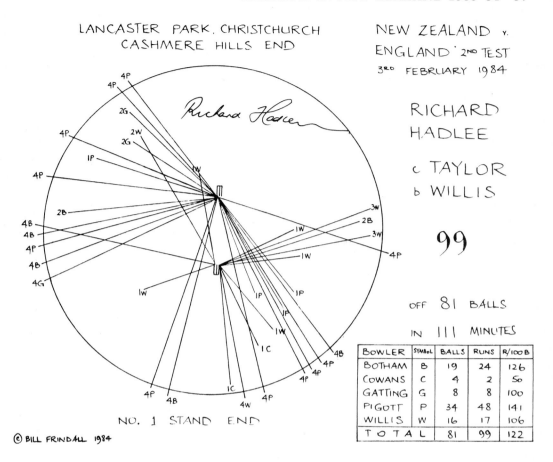

LANCASTER PARK, CHRISTCHURCH
CASHMERE HILLS END

NO. 1 STAND END

© BILL FRINDALL 1984

NEW ZEALAND v.
ENGLAND 2ND TEST
3RD FEBRUARY 1984

RICHARD HADLEE

c TAYLOR
b WILLIS

99

OFF 81 BALLS

IN 111 MINUTES

BOWLER	SYMBOL	BALLS	RUNS	R/100B
BOTHAM	B	19	24	126
COWANS	C	4	2	50
GATTING	G	8	8	100
PIGOTT	P	34	48	141
WILLIS	W	16	17	106
TOTAL		81	99	122

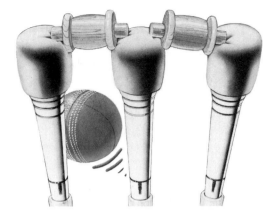

TMS IN PAKISTAN

———— Tony Lewis ————

The Test Match Special team gathered in Karachi for the second half of England's winter tour. New Zealand, the first part, had been a disaster. Not only had England lost a series there for the first time, but also certain players had been accused of pot-smoking and of licentious behaviour. The truth was to come out, so we were told as we set foot in the Holiday Inn, Karachi, the following weekend by the *Mail on Sunday* newspaper.

Don Mosey, the BBC's man on the tour, had been with these stories from the start. Michael Carey of the *Daily Telegraph* had, too, but he now swapped the Press box for the radio commentary boxes in Pakistan. From his usual Australian winter treadmill came the indomitable Henry Blofeld and with me from London arrived Jack Bannister, the former Warwickshire stalwart and cricket correspondent of the *Birmingham Post* and *Evening Mail*.

Some of the richest story-telling in cricket has come out of MCC tours of Pakistan and India. Back in the Thirties Alf Gover tells of how he ran up to bowl but made a hasty detour before reaching the umpire. He raced to the pavilion, leapt over sleeping bearers and crouching sweepers and locked himself in the lavatory. It can happen that quickly! The large crowd was even more astonished to see the skipper, the Hon. Lionel Tennyson, charge off the field after Gover, presenting himself in front of the lavatory door.

'Gover!' he shouted furiously.

Alf, realising that he had done the unforgivable of leaving the field without permission, mumbled abject apologies.

'Really am sorry, skipper. Got took short ... had this pain, y'know, just

DON MOSEY

Commentary from Lahore: Don Mosey, Henry Blofeld and local scorer.

under the waist-band ...'

'I'm not interested in your belly Gover. Give us the bleedin' ball back.'

More up-to-date are my own memories of a first trip to Pakistan in 1968. I was one of the Commonwealth side led by Richie Benaud. Accommodation was mainly in Rest Houses, and I recall sharing a room with David Allen, Roger Prideaux and John Murray. An old fan creaked on the ceiling, paint peeled from walls and there was no running water. Each morning a bearer came in with a bucket of pump water between the four of us. That was for washing, shaving, the lot. We tended to clean our teeth first! Every fourth day it was your own special treat; you would strip off and one of the others would throw the remains of the water over you. A shower day. Wonderful.

Now, 1984, the England team resides in the Holiday Inn Hotel in Karachi, one of the many five-star residences. Norman Gifford, the team's assistant manager, met me in the foyer and said, 'They don't know they're born do they ... but they won't have so much fun'. He was right.

As for the broadcasting in Pakistan, it is fair to write straight away how thoughtful and obliging were the colleagues of Radio Pakistan, even to the extent of laying on transport for us to and from the grounds.

Test Match Special, wherever it alights, is always running into local difficulties. In the Karachi commentary box the seats were made of hard, slatted plastic. I am afraid that our combined weight split them so that

'GIVE US OUR BLEEDIN' BALL BACK'

every time a commentator leaned forward to spot a player or to make an urgent point his buttocks would suffer a screaming Chinese pinch and the voice level would hit a sudden, misty peak. The ancient Vera Lynn microphones visibly flinched. Don Mosey turned to me one day for a comment, and it was in an effort to avoid the pinch that I leaned backwards not forwards, completely fracturing the back half of the seat. I disappeared down through the chair frame. Don was now interviewing a pair of feet! I made a strong physical effort to hoist myself back to microphone level but only succeeded in slipping lower. Silence struck the air waves. Vera Lynn could do nothing for me from that distance.

It was on the first day of the first Test Match in Karachi that Henry Blofeld demonstrated his unique art of commentating on views out of sight. He described a grand house on a hill beside the ground surrounded by palms, which you could see on the taxi ride in, but not at all from the commentary point itself.

'Yes. Surrounded by palms,' Henry informed the listeners to Radio 3 at home. 'Who owns it, I wonder?'

Next day there was a telegram to the ground from Scotland. It was from the former England batsman who has more yarns to spin about the sub-continent than any other I know, Peter Richardson, known to us all as Pakistan Pete. Henry was itching to read out the telegram but had to wait until he had supplied a minute's report for the 8.00 am news at home. It was one o'clock in the afternoon out there. Suddenly the line went dead. Henry could hear no news-reader and so had no idea when he was to build his brief up-date of play into his running commentary.

After a while he decided that the news would never come and so he launched out on his tale of the telegram. Unknown to him the news-reader in Broadcasting House in London, having just regaled the nation with the day's atrocities, thought Henry could still hear him and cued him thus:

NEWS-READER: 'Cricket, and on the second day of the First Test against Pakistan England were all out in their first innings this morning for 182. We are going over now to Henry Blofeld in Karachi for a report from the ground.'

BLOFELD FROM KARACHI UNWITTINGLY TO RADIO 2: 'No stroke and Taylor took ... well, Pakis ... er Peter Richardson, who's a very great friend of mine and Don Mosey too in this commentary team, and I am sure of the rest of us in this commentary team, says – we wanted to know ... and I myself suggested that some important official lived in this house and Majid Khan couldn't supply the answer ... and he says in his telegram, "Beautiful house surrounded by palms always owned by sahib in charge of tickets." Well (*chuckle, chuckle*), that may very well be. Anyway, Pete, very nice to hear from you and if you and your lovely wife Shirley are listening all the very best to you. (*Radio 2 news fades out in horror; listeners drop spoons in muesli.*)

LONDON NEWS-READER (*papers rustling*): 'And from cricket to er ... cricket

'... er ... er ... in ... er Guyana ...'

It was only 15 minutes later that we knew that Blowers' rambling thanks to Pakistan Pete had gone out live on the news between the world shaking information of the day.

When we were commentating loud and clear, we had to describe how England lost that Test Match at Karachi – Pakistan's first win over England in Pakistan. It was the result of deplorable England batting and fine bowling by the leg-spin, googly bowler, Abdul Qadir. He took 8 wickets in the match and only David Gower looked like managing an innings of any length.

The pitch did turn a lot and Nick Cook had a sensational match for England. His 6 for 65 and 5 for 18 would normally have been a match-winning performance, but Pakistan's first innings lead of 95 proved vital. Mohsin Khan passed 2,000 runs in Test cricket in this match.

Between the first and second Tests, on Sunday March 11th, the *Mail on Sunday* published their drug and sex story in London. The *Mail* had sent two reporters out to the team's hotel in Lahore to interview players. They assured players that the newspaper had sworn affidavits from New Zealand. The tour manager Alan Smith made a plain statement. 'As far as I know, our team has been well received and liked wherever we have been. ... I deplore attempts to unsettle members of the team.'

The newspaper ran their story for two weeks. Botham was said to be villain-in-chief and Lamb his most conspicuous ally. I record this because it seriously affected the relationship between the players and the media. The players were defensive, sullen, suspicious and basically unhappy. The cricket they played was poor. They became models of much-too-good behaviour. They were like Sunday School kids on an outing ... in a minefield.

At the Second Test, the Faisalabad Stadium was surprisingly beautiful, a neat concrete concourse outside, trim grass, car-parks, scooter-parks, cycle-parks, and a crisp architectural line to the stands – much more like the approach to Newbury Racecourse than to a cricket stadium in the sub-continent. The playing area is oval; the chamiana-covered stands are low, single-tier and elegant. The out-field grass is green; the pitch a grassless, biscuit brown. Our commentary point was perfect, between Pakistan TV and Radio. Unfortunately, the table which held the Vera Lynns was a step below our seats. One had to adopt the instant Quasimodo broadcasting position.

Willis was ill and did not play. Botham had gone home to have investigative surgery on his knee. Willis soon followed Botham and Gower captained. The match was drawn on a very good wicket but England did get runs. Gower led the way with 152, then Chris Smith got 66, Gatting 75, Randall 65 and Fowler 57. 546 for 8 declared: they had only one innings.

For Pakistan, Salim Malik confirmed his impressive form of the first Test by getting his third century in a brief international career. He plays sideways; his timing is fine and although quite relaxed in defence, he injects alarming power into his scoring strokes. This is a name for the future.

The final Test in Lahore was also drawn. Of the one-day internationals England won one, and Pakistan one.

It was Gower's 173 not out in the second innings at Lahore that prompted the question – is it time he captained England? The signs were good in the two Tests when he replaced Willis. He looked much more aware of cricket's possibilities in the field. He was inventive: England were scheming. However, it may be that Gower prospered because Botham and Willis were back in England. Botham is known as an unruly element in the team. Willis has never quite mastered the dual role of being the leading strike-bowler and the tactician. It was easier for Gower to be truly authoritative with his two former captains absent.

A huge cricketing question hangs over the tour too. Botham's potency as a medium-fast bowler has to be questioned. He is eminently an attacking force, but he does not look capable of bowling long spells as he once did under Brearley. Also, after the New Zealand rumours of bad behaviour, someone has to be bold enough to ask the question – is Botham's presence in the best interests of the side and of England cricket?

As radio commentators, we did not interfere with the players' private time, nor would we want to. Ideally the media should occupy a different hotel from the players ... not perfect for the purveyors of stories but best for the players.

And so we flew back with life itself *sub judice* because of the law suit initiated by Ian Botham against the *Mail on Sunday* newspaper. It made it a sad tour. Memorable, and rightly so, for Pakistan who won their first ever series against England, but supporters of England will recall only a tour in which the team got it wrong both on and off the field and dragged their reputations down.

As for the Test Match Special team, we enjoyed Pakistan and laughed at our usual gaffes. On my return a letter awaited me from Hywel ap Rees of St Ives, Steyning Road, Rottingdean, East Sussex.

'Dear Mr Lewis' it ran. '"Gower cracking Sarfraz's balls back past the bowler's ear for low skimming fours." Really! England cricket dies: Radio 3 lives.'

NIGHT OPERATIONS IN BROADCASTING HOUSE
'They also serve ...'
Peter Baxter

Setting off from deepest Hertfordshire on a January night always seems an incongruous way to start coverage of a day's play in a Test Match. But on just such a cold wet night my own winter campaign started. While, on the other side of the world on a sunlit New Zealand morning, England's cricketers were making their way through the streets of Wellington to the Basin Reserve ground, I was heading down the M1 towards Broadcasting House. Maybe I was no less apprehensive than they, as we were attempting something rather novel for Test Match Special.

Three weeks before I had seen Don Mosey off armed with a vast broadcasting schedule drawn up over the two months before Christmas. A daunting list for him to study on the plane bound for Fiji. An exhausting programme of telephone reports and studio sessions would leave him little time to himself, as I knew from my own experience – even without the commentaries. The New Zealand hours of play translated into Greenwich Mean Time made live commentary an unattractive proposition and, for that reason, something that we have never done from that country. Play starts at 10.00 pm GMT and finishes at 5.00 am. We would have liked to have carried the first session of each day (10.00 pm to midnight) but there was no network available to us at that time. So throughout the night Don would be providing telephone reports on the progress of the game and then, within an hour and a half of the close of play, we would be putting on a half-hour review of the day with commentary extracts supplied by Radio New Zealand. We usually rely on our opposite numbers for help, but this time RNZ would be the key to the success of the entire project.

The BBC Radio Sportsroom is not the most inspiring place to spend a night. By day it is full of bustling activity with the news agency tape-machines chattering, scripts rattling off typewriters and people in a world of their own concentrating on tape-recordings by means of headphones. Arriving in it at half past nine at night, though, to start a day's work one gets the feeling of 'after the Lord Mayor's show'. Wastepaper bins are overflowing, the day's football transfer news lies in a discarded heap of paper on one desk and a spike pierces a stack of rejected detail from the teleprinters. The first report of each day's play in New Zealand was for the last scheduled Radio 2 Sports Desk of the day at 9.55 pm. Contacting Don at that time was an anxious moment for me – not so much for the technical question of whether we would get through – but because the weather news he would have to impart was of crucial importance. Whatever happened we would have a half-hour programme to put on in the early morning and so we were always trying to prepare standby material against the day – by no means unknown in New Zealand – when there would be a complete washout. As it turned out, the only serious weather problems were in Christchurch where the Second Test gave us plenty of incident anyway. (Maybe England supporters would rather it had kept raining.) The technical side of things did intervene once at this time when Don Mosey's telephone line had been attacked by local gremlins and, despite the best endeavours of New Zealand Telecom engineers in a manhole outside the ground, it was midway through the day before we were in proper contact and by that time I had already had to leap into the Radio 2 studio to the surprise of the duty announcer to deliver an off-the-cuff appraisal of the current state of the game on the other side of the world. (A call to Radio New Zealand had, I must admit, given me a slight advantage in this.)

If events up to midnight were comparatively busy – Radio 4 and Radio 1 were still on the air and in the market for the latest score and sometimes even a report – after that time the night wore on with only hourly reports on Radio 2 as it soldiered through the small hours as ever. By this time I would have been joined by Joanne Watson and the script for the morning's Test Match Special would be taking shape slowly.

Joanne's is a voice known to followers of sport on Radio 2. A Yorkshire lass who bore the cracks of her colleagues over the problems and schisms in her county's cricket club during this winter cheerfully. She is no mean sportswoman herself, having played cricket for the Yorkshire juniors and hockey for Manchester University. Throughout the last three tours she has provided the vital – often unsung – production back-up which can make or break the tour coverage for the programmes that are taking contributions and for the isolated correspondent in the field.

A kettle and a jar of instant coffee, a tin of biscuits and – in my case – an often refilled pipe kept us alive through the graveyard shift. My script tried to allow for whatever might be provided at the end of the day in the way of commentary highlights as the progress was unfolded by our hourly conversations with Don. Questions like, 'Did Coney's 50 come before Hadlee was out?' were fired at him, and, puzzled as he may have been by their significance, he supplied the answers which helped the build-up of the jigsaw.

As 5.00 am approached, lethargy had to be shaken off and, while Joanne took the final live Radio 2 telephone report, the Test Match Special studio was making contact with Radio New Zealand to receive the day's highlights. Fortunately those at the other end were well alive to our need to record everything quickly and without fuss, and, after a fraught first day of the series as we both struggled to find our feet, the operation worked efficiently. With the last commentary extract received from the RNZ studio and already being licked into shape and matched up to the script, the line would be switched to the ground where Don would be ready to deliver the plethora of reports which the demands of four radio networks and even Breakfast Television impose on a tour correspondent. As these were recorded and despatched to their final destinations the clock would be ticking round inexorably towards 6.25 and Test Match Special's air time. It was a rude awakening for the two studio managers only roused from their beds an hour before, as the story of a day's cricket was assembled on little snippets of tape held together by a much altered and scribbled-on script. Joanne would be covering pieces of paper with sums of minutes and seconds to determine whether I would have to whistle for five minutes or talk at double speed.

The last five minutes rushed by and the red warning light flicked. No more time to polish or alter, the first drumbeats of our signature tune, 'Florida Fantasy', were sounding and we were on. As the grey dawn lightened the awakening streets of London we tried to enlighten Britain on the events which had taken place 13,000 miles away while they slept. Often, as I re-told the tale, I thought of players' wives perhaps waiting anxiously for news of their husbands' performances. Vanessa Tavaré in Kent dismayed at another single-figure score for Chris – sadly out of form on this tour; Liz Randall delighted at another haul of runs cheekily acquired by Derek. It can be a cruel game for those back home as well.

In the scramble of getting the programme on the air each morning, it is a remarkable tribute to Joanne and the excellence of the studio managers that I cannot remember any technical mishaps in the studio throughout what was an exacting series of programmes. Nonetheless we were relieved to get through it as the England team moved on to Pakistan and we moved into the attractions of live commentary.

The time difference between Britain and Pakistan is five hours which makes it, with India and Western Australia, ideal for the winter editions of Test Match Special. Play from lunch to the close would take us from 7.30 am to 11.30 – surely a good way to start a winter's morning at home. Our planning was slightly hindered by the decision of the Pakistani authorities to give devout Moslems at the matches a chance for their devotions on Fridays – the Mohammedan holy day. An hour and a half was set aside for lunch, giving a tremendous hiatus in the middle of the day's play which meant that the afternoon session did not start until 8.30 GMT. We only hoped that would-be listeners were not too confused – particularly as the first day of the series was a Friday.

The Pakistan leg of the tour, although a disastrous piece of cricket planning – a Test Match within two days of arriving and nothing but the three Tests and two one-day internationals – did have the benefit of being compact, confined mostly to the big centres and therefore attracting those who would make up our commentary team with Don Mosey – Tony Lewis, Henry Blofeld and Jack Bannister. Mike Carey was already on the tour for the *Daily Telegraph*.

For the tea intervals I had lined up Tony Cozier to give us regular reports on the series just starting between the West Indies and Australia. (There was one day when we could not make any contact with Trinidad where the Test was being played and so I tried another tack, ringing the Australian Broadcasting Corporation in Sydney. They supplied me with a report from their man on the tour, Jim Maxwell. By the time that went out on Test Match Special it had certainly travelled a few miles!) We also ran a couple of prize quizzes for the interval. I racked my brains for appropriate questions – not too difficult to frighten off all but the experts, yet, I hoped, interesting enough if you knew where to look up the answers. I hope they gave some fun. No prizes, but here is a small sample:

1. Ian Botham missed the Second Test in Faisalabad as he flew home with an injured knee. It would have given him a record 66th consecutive appearance for England. Where and when was the last previous Test that England played without him?
2. Twice in the Eighties a visiting team in England has had to call on a player not in the official tour party to make his Test debut. Who are the two? Which country was each playing for, and at which ground did each make his debut?
3. At the time of the Kerry Packer split in international cricket, who was Pakistan's captain and who took over the captaincy from him during the absence of the Packer players?
4. Test cricket has been played in which nine Pakistan cities? (One of them is no longer in Pakistan and another has had two different Test grounds.)

The answers are on page 50.

Having set the questions I then tried to devise a way for our commentators in Pakistan to be part of the drawing of the winners. Joanne and I drew out 20 correct cards at random from the great boxful we received, and numbered them. The commentators – after they, too, had been teased with the questions (none too easy if you did not have the chance to look them up) – called out two numbers and we had our winners.

Communications with the great sub-continent have always been a problem for broadcasters and we had a few days of anxiety, but not nearly so many as on our last series of commentaries from Pakistan, although the technicalities of the news bulletins for other networks which joined TMS for a score were sometimes fraught. The story of Henry Blofeld's dissertation on the palm-surrounded house in Lahore in the Radio 2 Saturday morning news is told elsewhere. That, we discovered later was caused simply by a faulty headphone lead at the ground, but there are always occasions when the circuit breaks down in one direction or the other.

On one heart-stopping morning it had become obvious that we were not being heard at the ground and we had already made alternative arrangements for news-scores. But in mid-commentary Don became suddenly disillusioned by the lack of any encouraging words in his headphones and announced to my horror that he saw no point in continuing since we had quite obviously lost all contact. Back in the studio I started talking, not knowing whether I would have to do so for 30 seconds or 30 minutes. Fortunately this hiatus spurred someone somewhere into curing the fault rapidly and I was spared too much floundering.

The longest break in the series came during the Third Test at Karachi. Annoyingly it happened just as David Gower had entered the 90s. After delivering the score-card and reading parish notices of decreasing importance, there was still no sign of the line and I resorted to music — Elgar's 'Nursery Suite'. No sooner was it playing than I saw how appropriate it was, as I looked through the studio window to see that my four-month-old daughter had been brought in for her first visit to a radio studio. She did not seem desperately impressed, so her mother took her shopping in Oxford Street (always a nerve-racking time for the finance department!). Meanwhile the music played on. There was, we discovered, a power failure in Karachi at the satellite station.

Eventually we were in contact again. Don was interrupted in the full flow of commentary which this time had continued regardless of the silence from London to allow us to rejoin him. It had been a 45-minute break. 'And has Gower got his hundred yet?' I asked.

'Good Lord, have you been away that long?' said a surprised Don. 'He got it over half an hour ago!'

Difficult mornings like these, when the circuit would disappear for just a few seconds at will, played havoc with the nerves. One did not dare relax, headphones were kept firmly clamped around ears and a note of the score was always to hand (not easy when some score-boards in Pakistan, it seemed from the commentary, were prone to subtract rather than to add). Not only the nerves suffered. The copious quantities of black coffee needed to keep me awake prompted the occasional need to dash down the corridor which had to be an opportunist desperate sprint with the risk of the network being plunged into silence.

Circuit breaks are a natural hazard. Less expected was Don's illness in Faisalabad. His capacity for survival in the most trying conditions is legendary. But one morning of the Second Test there was Henry Blofeld on the end of the line with the news that 'the Alderman' was stricken and in bed. The circumstances revealed a new and previously unrecognised talent in Henry who announced that he was running operations perfectly well at that end. The carefully worked out commentary rota had been adjusted and he appeared to have thought of all contingencies. Mutineers in his commentary box would, I had no doubt, be dealt with summarily.

The excitements of the last day of the series with Pakistan's run-chase abruptly halted by Cowans were felt as keenly in Studio 3B as in Karachi. We almost had to wash the dust from our throats when it was over and life could return to normal civilised time-keeping. With a new season on the way, several people were saying, 'I expect you'll be glad to be back with the cricket again soon. What do you do with yourself all winter?'

QUIZ ANSWERS
1. Karachi, January 1978
2. Mike Whitney for Australia at Old Trafford in 1981; Ehteshamuddin for Pakistan at Headingley in 1982
3. Mushtaq Mohammad before the split; Wasim Bari during it
4. Lahore (two grounds); Karachi; Faisalabad; Multan; Peshawar; Hyderabad; Rawalpindi; Bahawalpur; Dacca (now in Bangladesh).

ENGLAND TOUR OF NEW ZEALAND AND PAKISTAN 1983–84
Statistical Highlights   Bill Frindall

New Zealand v England
First Test – Wellington
Geoff Howarth, leading New Zealand for the eighteenth time in Tests, won his ninth toss and for the first time chose to bat.

Bob Willis took his 308th Test wicket when he dismissed Cairns and so overtook F. S. Trueman's tally to become England's leading wicket-taker.

Ian Botham achieved the double of a century and 5 wickets in an innings of the same Test for the fifth time. No one else has recorded this feat more than twice and A. W. Greig is the only other England player to complete it once.

Lance Cairns took the first 6 wickets to fall, including his 100th in Tests when he dismissed Lamb. His analysis of 7 for 143 was the best against England in New Zealand. In July 1983, Cairns had recorded the best analysis by a New Zealand bowler against England in either country: 7 for 74.

Jeremy Coney's 174 not out was the highest score of his career, the highest for New Zealand against England in New Zealand, the highest for New Zealand in all Tests at the Basin Reserve, and his first first-class 100 in 131 innings since 1977. His partnership of 118 with Cairns set a ninth-wicket record for New Zealand.

New Zealand's total of 537 was the highest in a Wellington Test by any side and their highest at home. It enabled them to extend their unbeaten run at Basin Reserve to nine Tests since 1968.

Second Test – Christchurch

For only the third time in 596 Tests England failed to include a specialist slow bowler. Both previous instances, against Australia at Melbourne in 1932–33 and at Brisbane in 1954–55, also resulted in defeat.

After compelling England to follow on for the first time (59 Tests), New Zealand gained their seventeenth victory (third against England) by their record margin of an innings and 132 runs. It was England's heaviest defeat since West Indies won by an innings and 226 runs at Lord's in 1973 and their first by an innings for 33 matches since Port-of-Spain in 1980–81.

England failed to total 100 in either innings for the first time since 1894–95. It was the fifteenth such instance in Test cricket (third by England) and the first since New Zealand were themselves England's victims in 1958.

Third Test – Auckland

Howarth became the first New Zealand captain to win three successive tosses in a home series.

John Wright and Jeff Crowe shared a fourth-wicket partnership of 154 to surpass the record against England set by 'Curly' Page and Roger Blunt at Lord's in 1931.

Ian Smith recorded his highest Test score for the fourth time in successive innings, and celebrated his maiden Test 100 by hitting the last 2 balls of the innings for 6 before uniquely catching Fowler off the next. He went on to make 5 dismissals to equal the New Zealand record.

New Zealand won their first series against England (and the Jordan Rose Bowl) at their twenty-first attempt in 54 years.

Pakistan v England
First Test – Karachi

Ian Botham played in his sixty-fifth consecutive Test, equalling England's record set by A. P. E. Knott. A knee injury compelled his return home before he could claim the record outright.

England's totals of 182 and 159 were their lowest in Pakistan (previously 191). Their first defeat in Pakistan ended a sequence of 11 draws and extended the home side's unbeaten record at Karachi to 21 Tests (10 wins).

Nick Cook's match analysis of 11 for 83 established a new England record in Pakistan, beating G. A. R. Lock's 8 for 225 at Dacca in 1961–62.

Second Test – Faisalabad

Salim Malik became only the third batsman after G. A. Headley and R. G. Pollock to score three Test 100s before his twenty-first birthday.

David Gower and Vic Marks added 167 for the seventh wicket to exceed the England record against Pakistan established by A. P. E. Knott and P. Lever at Birmingham in 1971. Gower's 100 was the first by an England captain since A. W. Greig scored 103 at Calcutta in 1976–77. He became the thirteenth to score 4,000 runs for England.

Third Test – Lahore

Mohsin Kamal became the hundredth player to represent Pakistan in Test Matches.

Sarfraz Nawaz scored his thousandth run in Tests during his highest innings (90) and was the third after Intikhab Alam and Imran Khan to complete the Test career double of 1,000 runs and 100 wickets for Pakistan.

Mohsin Khan and Shoaib Mohammad shared Pakistan's highest opening partnership against England, their 173 surpassing the record set by Shoaib's father, Hanif, and Alimuddin at Dacca in 1961–62.

Abdul Qadir (10 for 194) became the first to take more than 7 wickets for Pakistan in a home Test against England. His total of 19 wickets was a new Pakistan series record at home against England.

David Gower (449 runs) and Nick Cook (14 wickets) set new England series records in Pakistan.

Pakistan won their first series against England at their twelfth attempt in 30 years. For the first time England lost two Test series during the same season.

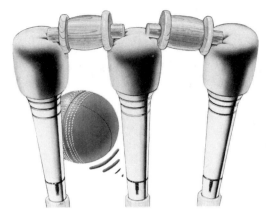

BLOWERS DOWN UNDER
Henry Blofeld

Australia has become a second home for me and when I landed in Sydney on Sunday October 16th 1983, it was my eleventh visit to the country. It was all gloriously familiar especially when my all-Australian taxi driver – unusual these days for they are mostly new Australians, usually from Greece – turned to me at a traffic light and said in ringing tones, 'What have you lot gone and done to Geoff Boycott then?' The Sunday papers proclaimed loudly on the battle for the Australian captaincy between Kim Hughes and Rod Marsh. I knew I was back.

The first ever five-Test series against Pakistan was unlikely to set Australian pulses racing too fast, but, when it was over, the beloved West Indies were to fly in to make up the third side for the one-day Benson and Hedges World Series Cup competition. It was a season for which the Packer-owned marketing arm of the Australian Cricket Board had found the disarming catch-phrase of 'Thunder Downunder'.

It looked like being muted thunder, for Pakistan's leading player and captain, Imran Khan, was unlikely to be fit. The stress fracture to his left shin had not healed properly and there was the likelihood that he would only be able to play as a batsman (as indeed happened).

While Australia won the series more easily than their 2-0 margin of victory suggested and the cricket as a contest was at times rather less than interesting, a great deal happened to make an amusing, intriguing and memorable summer. The domestic political problems which govern Pakistan cricket were seen at their most absurd and were a constant background to the action in Australia.

Abdul Qadir's leg-breaks had their moments; little Qasim Omar revealed himself as a potential winner of the Victoria Cross when it came to taking on Australia's fast bowlers; and, finally, Greg Chappell, Dennis Lillee and Rod Marsh all played their last Test Match for Australia, with Lillee keeping one last blazing row with the authorities going right to the end of his career.

I am still not sure that I fully understood the machinations of Pakistan's politicians or the exact course of all that happened in Lahore and Karachi, which succeeded only in undermining the team in Australia. It all began some time before the players left home when the selectors chose as captain Zaheer Abbas who had taken Pakistan to India in September, where by all accounts he had not done much of a job.

The Chairman of the Board of Control for Cricket in Pakistan, Air Marshall Nur Khan, immediately replaced Zaheer with Imran who had presumably assured the Air Marshall of his fitness, but apparently without producing any medical evidence in support. Imran then insisted on making some changes to the party, and one of those who had originally been chosen and was now left out was Shoiab Mohammad, the son of the Little Master, Hanif. Unwittingly, Shoiab had become a political hot potato because the chairman of the selectors, Haseeb Assan, who had picked the side for Australia was a permanent house guest of Shoiab's father, Hanif.

When Pakistan arrived in Brisbane for the first match of the tour, Imran saw a specialist who immediately prescribed a complete rest and no cricket for at least 15 days. This news brought howls of anguish from Karachi which supports Zaheer, the local boy – Imran's home is in Lahore – and petitions were sent to General Zia, the President of the country, demanding that Nur Khan be sacked. It was hardly the ideal start for Pakistan and not a ball had been bowled.

The tempo was maintained when a satisfying piece of scandal erupted in Australia. News came winging through from the west that Dennis Lillee had been offered the vice-captaincy of Western Australia which he had graciously accepted. Later that day, he was interviewed by Bob Maumill on Radio 6PR – the great man was not currently talking to the newspapers in Perth – and was asked if his acceptance meant that he had made it up with the state captain, Kim Hughes.

'Just because I have a drink with a bloke in the bar, it doesn't mean I am showing my sexual preferences,' came the illuminating reply.

Pakistan politics did not sit on the sidelines for long, for it soon became clear that without Imran's bowling Pakistan badly needed the services of Sarfraz Nawaz. Sarfraz had not been selected for the recent tour of India and had dared openly to criticise the selectors for failing to select him. For his pains he was banned from international cricket for six months by the BCCP. While we were in Adelaide for the South Australian game, news came through that Sarfraz had been officially reprieved and that his arrival was imminent.

The First Test in Perth was played on a green pitch: Pakistan's batsmen

were overwhelmed by Australia's four fast bowlers and Australia won by an innings. Wayne Phillips, lucky to play his first Test innings against such a poor attack, made 159 for Australia, but it was Qasim Omar's bravery which really stole the show. In the first innings he batted 150 minutes for 48 and never flinched once, although he was hit all over the body. When he was out he lay on the massage table in the pavilion while the Pakistan physio applied ice-packs to the worst of the bruises. Five were in place and as he approached with a sixth, Omar smiled up at him and said, 'Wouldn't it be better if I got into the fridge?'

At the Sydney Cricket Ground in the New South Wales game I saw the magnificent new electronic score-board in action for the first time. In the pavilion I came across Channel 9's newest commentator, actress Kate Fitzpatrick, interviewing Imran and brushing up on her leg-breaks and googlies. Then, on the Saturday evening I found myself with Imran at David Bowie's party at the Sebel Town House after a concert at the Showground. I am afraid I gave the hero a dreadful ear-bashing.

It was Pakistan politics again in Brisbane. It had become clear in Sydney after more medical advice that Imran was not going to be able to play until the Fourth Test and then only as a batsman. Just before the Second Test at the Gabba, word had come through from Pakistan that Zaheer had been appointed over Imran as the official tour captain. Zaheer's immediate reaction was to say that this was Imran's side and to summon Sarfraz and batsman Salim Malik from Pakistan. According to information at the time, the much harassed manager, Intikhab Alam, spent most of the night trying to track down Air Marshall Nur Khan for confirmation. He eventually ran him to ground in London and, by all accounts, Nur Khan instantly re-appointed Imran in between the pips.

When I arrived in Pakistan with the England side the following March, I was told that Zaheer had indeed been appointed, but that his most influential supporters in Karachi had got on to him in Brisbane and told him on no account to accept, for he was on a hiding to nothing. Their view was that this was Imran's side, it was going to be a disastrous tour in any event and Zaheer should keep his distance and allow Imran to take the blame. Accordingly, Imran was re-appointed. Rain prevented another Australian victory and when the Pakistanis flew into Melbourne they were met by the redoubtable Sarfraz whom the Pakistan authorities at home had located in Bombay.

Tennis was the game uppermost in many people's minds in Melbourne, for the Australian Open was being played at Kooyong where I spent a happy if rather wet day. At the Melbourne Cricket Ground, two 100s by Mudassar and one by Javed Miandad brought Pakistan a splendid victory after Victoria had batted for most of the first two days. It was my first glimpse of the splendid new Press box at the MCG which is both warm and comfortable. In Melbourne I joined Radio 3UZ's commentary team with former Victoria players Ian Meckiff, Ray Jordon and Jackie Potter in addition to John Mackinnon – and we all had a lot of fun in a jokey TMS sort of way.

Then it was Adelaide for the Third Test where the Pakistanis were joined by Salim Malik, to the surprise of some, since it was thought that, when Imran had returned to the captaincy in Brisbane, he had endorsed Sarfraz's invitation but had rescinded Salim's – I could never understand why Salim was not originally selected, for he is one of the outstanding young batsmen in the world. It was Sarfraz more than anyone who lifted Pakistan's performance in this match after a disastrous first day and enabled them to draw the match after taking them to a position from which they just might have won, but Abdul Qadir still insisted on bowling round the wicket to Australia's phalanx of left-handers. Qasim Omar made 100. Mohsin Khan made 150 and Lillee took 6 for 171 and gave a Press conference to wave two fingers at those who had been writing him off.

After a week's gentle cricket in Hobart in Tasmania – where at the Wrest Point Casino I made my customary annual donation to the croupier's benevolent fund – it was on to Melbourne for Christmas and the Fourth Test. Mohsin Khan made another big 100, Imran batted well and again Pakistan batted themselves into a position which could have brought victory. But Graham Yallop then made 200 and the straight bat and cool nerve of Imran steered Pakistan through to an anxious draw on the last day.

Remarkably, the series was therefore still undecided when the sides forgathered in Sydney for the Fifth Test. As it happened, the game was very one-sided with Australia winning by 10 wickets, but by the end it had become a truly momentous occasion.

The first act of note came on the first day when Greg Chappell caught Mudassar at second slip off Lawson and equalled Colin Cowdrey's record of 120 catches in Test cricket. Then, late on the second day, Sarfraz played forward to Lillee and was lbw giving Lillee his 350th Test wicket. Moments later when Rod Marsh caught Azeem Hafeez off Lillee he had taken his tally of Test dismissals to 350.

During the day, rumours of Greg Chappell's impending retirement had been circulating round the ground and now as he left the field he confirmed the news when interviewed by his brother Ian in front of the Channel 9 television cameras. I don't know whether Lillee's nose had been put out of joint by this news, but inside the pavilion he now decided that he was also going to call it a day.

By now Lillee was quite an expert at giving Press conferences and he gave another with considerable aplomb the next morning in the Noble Stand. He told us he was going to retire to a farm in the depths of Western Australia and enjoy the simple things of life. Greg Chappell then signed off with a magnificent innings of 182 while Lillee and Marsh both took the number of dismissals to 355 and Lillee's last was caught by Chappell which took him past Cowdrey's record. It was a fairy-tale ending for all of them.

Earlier days for the Chappells and Marsh – discussing tour selections in England in 1975.

By now the West Indies were with us as we set off on the helter-skelter round Australia for the Benson and Hedges Cup. The Pakistan authorities at home had refused to send left-arm spinner Iqbal Qasim to join the beleaguered team for the Fifth Test but off-spinner Ejaz Fakih now mysteriously appeared while reserve wicket-keeper Ashraf Ali, who had been scheduled to return home, was still with us. The West Indies won the one-day competition although, extraordinarily, they were overwhelmed by Pakistan in one of the early matches.

The West Indies easily beat Australia in the first final, the second was a most exciting tie and then the ACB persuaded the West Indians of the necessity of playing a third final in order to take advantage of a huge Sunday gate at the MCG. The third game was necessary only if the two sides were level after the first two games, when in fact the West Indies were already one match ahead. Even if Australia had won the third game, the West Indies would still have won the competition since they had won more of the preliminary matches. It was an extraordinary decision by the Board and one which the Melbourne public saw through, for only 20 thousand people turned up.

Lillee's final transgression came in a Sheffield Shield game in Brisbane when he was captaining Western Australia. Although one session in which WA were fielding was shortened by 45 minutes' rain, Lillee still demanded a drink interval. The umpires refused to let him have it, but he insisted, and took it. The ACB disciplinary committee made him pay a suspended fine of a thousand dollars imposed a year before and suspended him from WA's two remaining games. Lillee then applied for an injunction so that the case should be heard in the Supreme Court. The delay would have meant he could have played in those last two games. But the judge threw the case out, saying that umpires had to be obeyed. Lillee had bitten the dust at last and maybe it was a good point at which to end the season.

AUSTRALIA V PAKISTAN 1983–84
Statistical Highlights   Bill Frindall

First Test – Perth
Wayne Phillips, South Australia's 25-year-old left-handed opening batsman, became the ninth to score 100 in his first innings for Australia. His second-wicket partnership of 259 with Grahame Yallop established an all-wicket record for either country in this series.

Carl Rackemann's match analysis of 11 for 118 in his second Test was an Australian record against Pakistan in either country and the best by any bowler in a Test at the WACA Ground.

Second Test – Brisbane
Rodney Hogg became the twentieth Australian to take 100 wickets in Test Matches when he dismissed Mohammad Nazir in the first innings.

Allan Border and Greg Chappell shared a partnership of 171 to equal the fifth-wicket record by either country in this series.

Third Test – Adelaide

Pakistan's total of 624 was the highest by either country in this series, their second highest in all Tests, the fifth highest by any country against Australia, and the highest in all Tests since 1979, when England scored 633 for 5 declared against India at Edgbaston. It was also the highest total against Australia since 1938 when England compiled their world record 903 for 7 declared at The Oval.

The partnerships of 233 by Mohsin Khan and Qasim Omar and 186 by Javed Miandad and Salim Malik were Pakistan records for the second and fifth wickets respectively against Australia.

The match aggregate of six individual centuries was one short of the record for any Test.

Fourth Test – Melbourne

Grahame Yallop's score of 268 was the highest for either country in this series and the third highest by any batsman against Pakistan. It took him past 1,000 runs for the Australian season before January, a feat achieved previously only by W. H. Ponsford, H. Sutcliffe, R. B. Simpson (twice), G. Boycott and D. W. Hookes. The highest innings of his first-class career, it took his aggregate for the calendar year 1983 to 1,834, surpassing D. G. Bradman's record for Australian first-class cricket (1,763 in 1929). Batting for 167 minutes, he played the sixth longest innings in all first-class cricket, the third longest for Australia in Tests, and the longest for a score of under 300.

Yallop's partnerships of 203 with Kim Hughes and 185 with debutant Greg Matthews established Australian third- and seventh-wicket records respectively against Pakistan.

Imran Khan became the fifth player to complete the double of 2,000 runs and 200 wickets in Test cricket.

Fifth Test – Sydney

Greg Chappell became the sixth batsman to score 7,000 runs in Test cricket and passed D. G. Bradman's Australian record of 6,996. He also emulated the feats of fellow Australians R. A. Duff and W. H. Ponsford by scoring 100 in both his first and his last Test. He later broke M. C. Cowdrey's world record of 120 catches by a fielder in Test matches, finishing with a total of 122.

Dennis Lillee and Rodney Marsh, each playing in his final Test, became the first to take 350 wickets and make 350 dismissals in Test cricket respectively. Both finished with totals of 355, a world record 95 of them being shared (*ct* Marsh *b* Lillee).

Wasim Bari, also making his last Test appearance, became the third wicket-keeper after Marsh and A. P. E. Knott to take 200 catches in Tests.

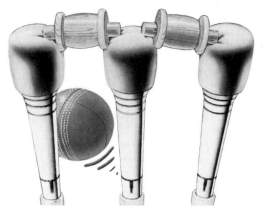

WEST INDIES IN ENGLAND 1984

The First Test at Edgbaston
Christopher Martin-Jenkins

The enthusiasm with which I always look forward to the first Test Match of any series was tempered on this occasion by the fact that I had agreed to make one of the only two speeches at a major dinner to be given at Edgbaston on the evening before the game. It is not always possible to put as much time into the preparation of after-dinner speeches as I would like but this time I had worked hard in advance, partly because there would be many people I knew present and also because, with over 1,100 people there, it was an important occasion for the newly formed West Midlands branch of the Lord's Taverners who raise such vast sums each year to provide facilities both for young cricketers and for physically handicapped people.

Fortunately, Bob Bevan, who made the hilarious second speech, and I were generously received and, although it might seem more daunting talking to a thousand plus people than to say, fifty, it is, in fact, much easier provided one gets off the mark with a couple of good shots early on.

The only mishaps during the evening occurred when on several occasions the lights failed (including one in the middle of my peroration) and when it started to rain heavily outside, causing a cascade of water to pour through a gap in the roof of the marquee: neither event was calculated to aid the concentration of either speaker or listeners but happily, nothing could spoil the pervading air of merriment.

There was no more rain around when Thursday dawned, warm and over-cast. It was no surprise to find a sizeable crowd assembling when I reached the ground at 10.15. I had bumped into Jim Cumbes, the 'much travelled' fast-medium bowler, now commercial manager of Warwickshire, at a couple of cricket dinners during the winter and he had mentioned that he had had no difficulty at all in selling the many facilities Edgbaston has to offer to businessmen wanting to watch a Test Match in comfort, with food and drink laid on. The attraction, of course, was not the food and drink but the fact that firstly this was 'The Edgbaston Test', still, for all the proliferation of Tests around the world in recent years, a real occasion for Birmingham folk, and secondly the visitors were the West Indies, by some distance the best cricket team in the world.

Clive Lloyd's team of all the talents now had an off-spinner in Roger Harper to add to the four fast bowlers and, although their batting generally was marginally more suspect than it had been in 1976 – the last occasion when the weather had allowed them to display their full range of talents under an English heaven – the evidence of the three Texaco internationals was that Viv Richards, scare stories of an eye disease now forgotten, was if possible even better than he was when amassing 829 runs in four Tests in that season of drought. As for the bowling, it was certainly stronger now than in 1980, when Parry, an under-estimated off-spinner, ought to have been used but was not (admittedly Harper is more of an all-rounder and Dujon a better bat than Murray, thus lengthening the batting). In the First Test of 1976, the main West Indies bowlers were Roberts, Daniel, Julien and Holder, supported at various times during a drawn match at Trent Bridge by Fredericks, Lloyd, Richards, Gomes and Kallicharran. At other times during that series, which West Indies won 3–0, Collis King did some bowling and two specialist spinners, Albert Padmore and Raphick Jumadeen, also had a game each. In other words the idea of a full-scale battery of fast bowling had not yet been fully evolved but, by the last Test at The Oval, Lloyd had chosen four specialists: Holding, Roberts, Daniel and Holder.

By 1984, Holding was no longer taking the new ball, Holder had retired and Roberts and Daniel were still at large in county cricket, having given way to the new wave. Small and Walsh had not been picked for this opening Test at Edgbaston but Marshall, Garner, Holding and Baptiste knew that any loss of fitness, form or fury would let one of them into the team.

Above all, in all senses of that term, West Indies now had Joel Garner. The giant had returned refreshed from a rest to overwhelm Australia in the Caribbean in March and April, and Englishmen in Somerset and beyond were amazed and afeared to see him running in during the early games of this tour faster than ever before.

With both Garner and Richards performing at their peak and Lloyd

A sickening blow at Edgbaston. Andy Lloyd is felled by Malcolm Marshall.

batting as well as ever, it was obvious to us all that England were going to need quite extraordinary luck to offer their opponents a serious challenge. I personally felt that only an injury to one or more of these three key West Indians, Lloyd, Richards and Garner, would let England in with a chance. In the event all three played vital parts at Edgbaston, Lloyd making 71 in no time and controlling his bowlers and fielders with confident dexterity, Richards making 117 despite feeling unwell, and Garner taking 9 wickets.

The first morning of the match was disastrous for England and, to some extent, set the pattern for the whole series. Garner quickly got rid of Fowler and of Randall, who had come back from another successful tour but was obviously ill at ease at number three. The crucial moment of the morning, however, was when Andy Lloyd, the perky and pleasant Shropshire lad who had made an encouraging start to his Test career, was hit just above the right eye by a ball from the whippy Barbadian, Malcolm Marshall. I was on the air at the time and had the unpleasant task of describing the way that Lloyd, having misjudged the height of the bounce and the length of the ball, tried in vain to pull his head back out of line and, having been hit, fell like a shot partridge beside the stumps. Though there was a long delay before the stunned Lloyd got to his feet he was seriously considering batting on. But his vision was badly blurred by the bruising behind the eye, and wiser counsels, from Bernard Thomas, prevailed. He walked off on his way to a fortnight in hospital and a long absence from cricket.

Lloyd said later that he was very relieved that he had been wearing a helmet even though he had been cut when the transparent plastic protector, which comes down beside the peak of the helmet, dug into the flesh. Whether or not helmets should be worn is still something of a contentious point. One can absolutely understand *why* they are worn but no one can deny that since they have come into general use in first-class cricket more and more players have been hit. This may be partly because batsmen wearing helmets, whether they be tailenders or not, are considered fair game for bouncers by fast bowlers. It may also be that the feeling of security offered by helmets persuades batsmen to play shots they would otherwise not try. But it is my impression that at least as many batsmen are being hit when ducking as they are when hooking. For some reason more players are taking their eyes off the ball when danger threatens. The lesson of Lloyd's injury, and of several others, may have been that helmets need to be even stronger and more genuinely protective, along the lines of those unlovely things worn by American footballers. If protection is going to be worn, it might as well be really strong.

It was certainly noticeable during this series how few of the West Indies batsmen wore helmets but, although Tony Cozier pointed out that they were seldom worn in club cricket in the Caribbean, despite all the fast bowlers around, it might have been a different story if the West Indians had been confronted by their own fast bowlers.

By lunch England were 73 for 4, but because of Lloyd's injury, they were actually 5 wickets down. Fortunately there was some tougher resistance forthcoming in the afternoon from Ian Botham, who hit some fine shots, and Paul Downton, who showed exemplary technique and an ideal temperament. Downton had been picked ahead of various other possible wicket-keeping candidates, including Bob Taylor, David Bairstow, Jack Richards and Bruce French. Both as batsman and wicket-keeper, Downton was to justify his choice throughout the series and it was undoubtedly a realistic decision to pick him ahead of Bob Taylor. Nevertheless, it was sad to see Taylor dropped after a successful winter tour in which he had given his usual flawless performances behind the stumps and had behaved, by all accounts, with his customary good grace. Bob was always the ideal team man and perfect ambassador. He said when he got back that he had felt a certain generation gap between himself and some of the less dedicated professionals in the team.

England were all out soon after tea on the first day but they had the consolation, before the end of the day, of getting rid of both the West Indies openers, Greenidge and Haynes, both trapped lbw by 'nip-backers' from the deposed captain, Bob Willis.

I was staying during the match at the Belfry Hotel, which apart from being a very pleasant watering-hole also serves as the club-house for two purpose-built golf courses, the Brabazon and the Derby, where the PGA have their headquarters and where the 1985 Ryder Cup is due to be played. The Brabazon is much too daunting a course for an amateur hacker like me, but the Derby is fairly bland and straightforward and I had a few holes with John Thicknesse of the *Standard* on a lovely sunny evening before supper. I was anxious to hit a few shots, having not played since the previous summer and rather rashly agreed to take part in an early morning game on Friday. The venue was Walsall, where my partner was Jack Bannister, the former Warwickshire bowler, now a prominent cricket pundit, as well as being a successful bookmaker and an ideal Secretary of the Cricketers' Association. He is also a very steady golfer, much more so than I am, and on his home course he was a good man to have on one's side. Unfortunately one of our opponents was another, even better, member of the home club, Alan Smith (not A.C. of Oxford, Warwickshire and England) and the other was Richie Benaud – *the* Richie Benaud. He looks and plays much like a professional and his partner was almost faultless so Bannister and Jenkins did not take home much money.

Eighteen holes of golf was certainly a good way to set oneself up for a day's commentaries and there was plenty of good batting to watch and describe as Richards and Gomes scored excellent 100s to give the West Indies a firm grip on the First Test.

Richards, in fact, took complete control after lunch and Gomes suffered little by comparison, playing beautifully straight and certainly not shy to play his strokes as he had sometimes been on previous visits to England. Nick Cook took some terrible stick from Richards and must have been mightily relieved when at last he hit him in the air to a fielder.

Gomes batted on well into the final session in which the England bowlers began to have some real success. It would have been very interesting to see whether they could have finished the job that night had they been able to bowl another 10 overs as they would have been forced to do if the West Indies had agreed to a minimum number of 96 overs in the day.

After play on that Friday I attended the garden party which Bernard Thomas kindly hosts on the second evening of each Edgbaston Test at his sumptuous remedial clinic in Somerset Road. On a warm, sultry evening the gardens were looking lovely, the array of cheeses had to be seen to be believed, both for size and variety, and the company was convivial. Amongst those I spoke to, apart from some of the cricketers of both teams, was the former Minister for Sport, Denis Howell, Chairman of the Birmingham Sporting Club who were giving the party, and an Olympic hockey player shortly off to Los Angeles to represent Great Britain. He had mixed feelings about the fact that he was going only because of the boycott of the games by the Communist countries. Oh, for sport without politics!

The West Indies took embarrassingly total control of the game on the Saturday, another hot day. At first it was just muggy, with no sunshine, ideal for swing bowling and in his bowling prime I suspect Ian Botham would have made short work of the tail. But he has lost pace and the out-swingers now tend to be of the banana variety rather than the really dangerous type which nip away from a groping bat at the last moment. At the other end Pringle bowled a good line and length but seldom moved the ball in the air. Having taken one wicket Pringle, along with Botham and all the other England bowlers, became like prompters on the side of the stage as Baptiste and Holding bestrode its centre like Olivier and Gielgud. We all knew that in other circumstances Baptiste and Holding were, as batsmen, really only moderate repertory players, but far from strutting and fretting for one inconsequential hour, they dominated the scene for more than two.

In the end, the West Indies totalled 606 and, by the end of Saturday's play, with Garner bowling fast and formidably well, England had lost four of their ten fit batsmen. Only Downton, opening in place of Lloyd, had the necessary combination of sound technique, courage, concentration, self-discipline and luck to survive.

I spent Saturday evening with a Cambridge friend, David Gower – no relation – and his family. His two sons are in the same prep school Under 11 team as the sons of Dennis Amiss and Alvin Kallicharran.

Had I not had a mortgage and school fees to pay I would have been playing cricket rather than watching it on Sunday but bills cannot be ignored, whether they be of the Frindall variety or any other, so I sped down motor-ways to Cardiff. A glorious drive it was, too. The Herefordshire/Monmouth-shire area is one part of the country I hardly know but you could not imagine more lovely countryside. On the way back I even left the motorway to make a more leisurely inspection. But I was very weary when I finally got back to the Belfry and next year I shall actually try to rest on the rest day.

Monday was another lovely, sunny day and no one wanted the match to end too soon, though everyone had booked out of their hotel rooms in the certain knowledge that they would be homeward bound a day early. In the event Downton reached his admirable 50 and Pringle, with the match all but over, only just missed his, but soon after lunch we were on our way, wondering if there was any combination of available English players capable of beating Clive Lloyd's immensely powerful team. Rather than dwell on England's many shortcomings at Edgbaston it was better to think instead what a brilliant side it was which had just thrashed them out of sight.

ENGLAND 1ST INNINGS v. WEST INDIES at EDGBASTON, BIRMINGHAM (1ST TEST) on 14,15,16,18 JUNE 1984.

Toss: ENGLAND

IN	OUT	MINS	No.	BATSMAN	HOW OUT	BOWLER	RUNS	WKT	TOTAL	6s	4s	BALLS	NOTES ON DISMISSAL
11·00	11·07	7	1	G. FOWLER	C' DUJON	GARNER	0	1	1	·	·	9	Vicious lifter - simple catch off glove
11·00	11·33	33	2	T.A. LLOYD	RETIRED HURT		10	(2)	20	·	1	17	Ducked into lifting ball - hit on side of helmet - bowled by Marshall. Hospitalised - vision blurred - cut above right temple.
11·09	11·15	6	3	D.W. RANDALL	BOWLED	GARNER	0	2	5	·	·	3	Played on - middled backfoot defensive stroke rebounded
11·17	12·30	73	4	D.I. GOWER *	C' HARPER	HOLDING	10	4	49	·	1	49	3rd slip - cut at wide long hop.
11·35	12·17	42	5	A.J. LAMB	C' LLOYD	BAPTISTE	15	3	45	·	2	32	Edged low to 1st slip. Excellent catch - dived forward.
12·19	3·23	144	6	I.T. BOTHAM	C' GARNER	HARPER	64	7	168	·	10	82	Mismored lofted drive - skier to mid-off. (HIS HS v. WEST INDIES)
12·32	1·55	43	7	G. MILLER	C' DUJON	GARNER	22	5	89	·	4	43	Low, right-handed catch - very well-judged - defensive stroke.
1·57	2·10	13	8	D.R. PRINGLE	C' DUJON	HOLDING	4	6	103	·	1	7	Back defensive stroke - edged lifting offside ball.
2·11	4·22	110	9	P.R. DOWNTON †	LBW	GARNER	33	9	191	·	3	101	HS in TESTS. Played back - beaten by breakback.
3·25	3·41	16	10	N.G.B. COOK	C' LLOYD	MARSHALL	2	8	173	·	·	15	Edged defensively to 1st slip - held at third attempt.
4·02	(4·22)	20	11	R.G.D. WILLIS	NOT OUT		10			·	1	12	(800 TEST MATCH RUNS when 3) 53rd not out (world Test record)

* CAPTAIN   † WICKET-KEEPER

| EXTRAS | b 8 | lb 5 | w - | nb 8 | 21 | - 23 370 balls (including 13 no balls) |

TOTAL (59·3 OVERS, 261 MINUTES) 191 all out at 4·22 pm on 1st day.

13 OVERS 4 BALLS/HOUR
3·21 RUNS/OVER
52 RUNS/100 BALLS

BOWLER	O	M	R	W	nb	HRS	OVERS	RUNS
MARSHALL	14	4	37	1	4	1	12	39
GARNER	14·3	2	53	4	7	2	14	34
HOLDING	16	4	44	2	-	3	14	66
BAPTISTE	11	3	28	1	2	4	14	34
HARPER	4	1	8	1	-			
							21	
	59³	14	191	9				

RUNS	MINS	OVERS	LAST 50 (in mins)
50	94	19·3	94
100	148	32·1	54
150	192	43·0	44

LUNCH: 73-4   BOTHAM 12* (41 min)
MILLER 12* (28 min)
OFF 26 OVERS IN 120 MINUTES

TEA: 173-8   DOWNTON 25* (90 min)
OFF 54·3 OVERS IN 241 MINUTES

WKT	PARTNERSHIP		RUNS	MINS
1st	Fowler	Lloyd	1	7
2nd	Lloyd	Randall	4	6
3rd	Lloyd Lamb	Gower	15 25	33 42
4th	Gower	Botham	4	11
5th	Botham	Miller	40	43
6th	Botham	Pringle	14	13
7th	Botham	Downton	65	72
8th	Downton	Cook	5	16
9th	Downton	Willis	18	20
10th			191	

Compiled by BILL FRINDALL

WEST INDIES 1ST INNINGS — IN REPLY TO ENGLAND'S 191 ALL OUT

IN	OUT	MINS	No.	BATSMAN	HOW OUT	BOWLER	RUNS	WKT	TOTAL	6s	4s	BALLS	NOTES ON DISMISSAL
4·36	5·28	52	1	C.G. GREENIDGE	LBW	WILLIS	19	2	35	·	3	47	Played back - sharp breakback.
4·36	5·24	48	2	D.L. HAYNES	LBW	WILLIS	8	1	34	·	1	24	Played back - sharp breakback. (ct off no ball previous ball.)
5·26	5·49	380	3	H.A. GOMES	C⁴ MILLER	PRINGLE	143	5	418	1	16	279	6th in TESTS; (1st v ENGLAND. HS in TESTS. Edged to 1st slip.
5·30	2·35	204	4	I.V.A. RICHARDS	C⁴ RANDALL	COOK	117	3	241	1	17	154	5000 RUNS when 13. (17th in TESTS; 7th v ENGLAND. Drove to mid-off.
2·37	4·03	64	5	P.J. DUJON †	C⁴ GOWER	MILLER	23	4	294	·	2	51	Edged off-break via pad to silly-point.
4·05	5·53	108	6	C.H. LLOYD *	C⁴ PRINGLE	BOTHAM	71	6	418	·	8	89	Edged outswinger (from round the wicket) to 1st slip.
5·51	5·59	8	7	M.D. MARSHALL	LBW	PRINGLE	2	7	421	·	·	5	Hit across line. Slower ball.
5·55	11·40	44	8	R.A. HARPER	BOWLED	PRINGLE	14	8	455	·	3	31	Missed lofted straight drive.
11·00	(2·18)	161	9	E.A.E. BAPTISTE	NOT OUT		87			·	11	131	HS in TESTS.
11·42	2·13	114	10	M.A. HOLDING	C⁴ WILLIS	PRINGLE	69	9	605	4	8	80	HS in TESTS. Hooked bouncer to long-leg. 50 off 43 BALLS.
2·15	2·18	3	11	J. GARNER	C⁴ LAMB	PRINGLE	0	10	606	·	·	6	Edged low to 3rd slip.

* CAPTAIN   † WICKET-KEEPER   EXTRAS   b 6 lb 17 w 2 nb 28   53   5s 69s 897 balls (including 39 no balls)

TOTAL (143 OVERS, 601 MINUTES)   606 all out at 2·18 pm 3rd day

(LEAD: 415)

14 OVERS 1 BALLS/HOUR
4·24 RUNS/OVER
68 RUNS/100 BALLS

BOWLER	O	M	R	W		HRS	OVERS	RUNS
WILLIS	25	3	108	2	3/4	1	12	41
BOTHAM	34	7	127	1	-1/2	2	12	52
PRINGLE	31	5	108	5	15/4	3	14	48
COOK	38	6	127	1	-4	4	17	70
MILLER	15	1	83	1	-6	5	16	69
			53			6	16	61
	143	22	606	10		7	12	67
						8	14	89
						9	14	89
						10	16	62

2ND NEW BALL taken at 4·36 pm 2nd day — WEST INDIES 341-4 after 86 overs.

RUNS	MINS	OVERS	LAST 50 (in mins)
50	69	13·3	69
100	131	26·5	62
150	193	41·5	62
200	229	52·3	36
250	271	62·3	42
300	332	78·1	61
350	369	88·2	37
400	410	97·1	41
450	475	112·0	65
500	518	121·4	43
550	543	128·1	25
600	590	140·3	47

STUMPS: 53-2 GOMES 4* (34 min) RICHARDS 14* (30 min)
(1st DAY) OFF 17 OVERS IN 84 MINUTES

LUNCH: 159-2 GOMES 48* (154 min) RICHARDS 66* (150 min)
OFF 45 OVERS IN 204 MINUTES

TEA: 293-3 GOMES 102* (273 min) DUJON 23* (63 min)
OFF 76 OVERS IN 333 MINUTES

STUMPS: 421-7 HARPER 0* (4 min)
103·3 OVERS IN 440 MIN

LUNCH: 578-8 BAPTISTE 72* (123 min) HOLDING 60* (81 min)
OFF 133 OVERS IN 563 MINUTES

WKT	PARTNERSHIP		RUNS	MINS
1st	Greenidge	Haynes	34	48
2nd	Greenidge	Gomes	1	2
3rd	Gomes	Richards	206	204
4th	Gomes	Dujon	53	64
5th	Gomes	Lloyd	124	104
6th	Lloyd	Marshall	0	2
7th	Marshall	Harper	3	4
8th	Harper	Baptiste	34	40
9th	Baptiste	Holding	150	114
10th	Baptiste	Garner	1	3

‡ WEST INDIES 9th WKT RECORD v ENGLAND.
606
Compiled by BILL FRINDALL

ENGLAND 2ND INNINGS — 415 BEHIND ON FIRST INNINGS

IN	OUT	MINS	No.	BATSMAN	HOW OUT	BOWLER	RUNS	WKT	TOTAL	6s	4s	BALLS	NOTES ON DISMISSAL
2·32	3·18	46	1	G. FOWLER	LBW	GARNER	7	1	17	·	·	40	Late on stroke - shuffled across stumps.
2·32	12·29	276	2	P.R. DOWNTON †	C⁴ GREENIDGE	HARPER	56	7	181	·	3	187	HS in TESTS. Edged off-break via pad to silly point.
3·20	3·28	8	3	D.W. RANDALL	C⁴ LLOYD	GARNER	1	2	21	·	·	9	Top-edged cut to 1st slip.
3·30	4·07	16	4	D.I. GOWER *	C⁴ DUJON	GARNER	12	3	37	·	1	17	Top-edged cut to 'keeper.
4·09	5·45	49	5	A.J. LAMB	C⁴ RICHARDS	MARSHALL	13	4	65	·	1	32	Edged backfoot offside force to 2nd slip. Misjudged bounce.
5·00	11·20	80	6	I.T. BOTHAM	LBW	GARNER	38	5	127	1	4	66	Beaten by breakback that kept low.
11·22	11·34	12	7	G. MILLER	C⁴ HARPER	MARSHALL	11	6	138	·	1	10	Gloved bouncer via helmet to 3rd slip - simple catch.
11·36	(1·56)	101	8	D.R. PRINGLE	NOT OUT		46			·	5	88	-
12·31	12·47	16	9	N.G.B. COOK	RUN OUT (GOMES)		9	8	193	·	1	12	Backed up - failed to regain ground - direct throw from mid-on.
12·49	1·56	28	10	R.G.D. WILLIS	C⁴ DUJON	GARNER	22	9	235	·	3	13	Followed offside ball.
			11	T.A. LLOYD	ABSENT HURT								Detained in hospital with blurred vision in right eye.

* CAPTAIN   † WICKET-KEEPER   EXTRAS   b 1 lb 5 w 4 nb 10   20   1s 19s 474 balls (including 13 no balls)

TOTAL (76·5 OVERS, 324 MINUTES)   235 all out at 1·56 pm on 4th day

14 OVERS 1 BALLS/HOUR
3·06 RUNS/OVER
50 RUNS/100 BALLS

BOWLER	O	M	R	W		HRS	OVERS	RUNS
MARSHALL	23	7	65	2	3/4	1	14	27
GARNER	23·5	7	55	5	3/-	2	14	37
HOLDING	12	3	29	0	3/-	3	13	40
HARPER	13	3	48	1		4	14	42
BAPTISTE	5	1	18	0	2/4	5	15	49
			20	1				
	76·5	21	235	9				

RUNS	MINS	OVERS	LAST 50 (in mins)
50	89	20·3	89
100	171	39·2	82
150	238	55·2	67
200	300	70·3	62

TEA: 32-2 [16 OVERS / 68 MIN.] DOWNTON 12* (68 min) GOWER 8* (10 min)

STUMPS: 112-4 [43 OVERS / 187 MIN.] DOWNTON 34* (187 min) BOTHAM 30* (60 min)
(3RD DAY)   303 BEHIND

LUNCH: 221-8 [73 OVERS / 309 MIN.] PRINGLE 35* (86 min) WILLIS 19* (13 min)
194 BEHIND

WEST INDIES WON BY INNINGS & 180 RUNS
(ONLY THE SECOND ENGLAND DEFEAT AT EDGBASTON)

MAN OF THE MATCH: H.A. GOMES
(Adjudicator: F.S. Trueman)

TOTAL TIME LOST: NIL

WKT	PARTNERSHIP		RUNS	MINS
1st	Fowler	Downton	17	46
2nd	Downton	Randall	4	8
3rd	Downton	Gower	16	16
4th	Downton	Lamb	28	49
5th	Downton	Botham	62	80
6th	Downton	Miller	11	12
7th	Downton	Pringle	43	53
8th	Pringle	Cook	12	16
9th	Pringle	Willis	42	28
·			235	

Compiled by BILL FRINDALL

The Second Test at Lord's
Trevor Bailey

A Lord's Test is much more than just another cricket match. Over the years it has gradually acquired a special atmosphere, tradition and importance, so that, along with Wimbledon and Henley, it has become one of the summer's great national sporting occasions. This is the game in which every touring player wants to take part and which produces easily the biggest gate receipts for the county clubs.

Lord's saw a happy debut for Nottinghamshire's Chris Broad and, after his successful first Test innings, he was hauled up to our commentary area at the top of the pavilion to be interviewed for the Radio 2 Sports Desk by Don Mosey. His enthusiasm for the whole atmosphere of Test cricket in which he was revelling was obvious as he came into the Test Match Special box just to sit and listen. When he shook hands with Brian Johnston we thought it was their first meeting, but Chris revealed that as a small boy at a match at Bristol he had asked for – and got – Brian's autograph. And so, 15 or so years later, Brian did the decent thing and asked Chris for his autograph. 'I promise I shan't swap it', he assured him.   **P.B.**

As the headquarters of the game, Lord's also attracts more cricket-lovers from overseas than any of our other Test grounds, and these do not only come from the country of the touring party. At the Lord's Cornhill Test against the West Indies, I met friends from Australia, India, Pakistan, South Africa, New Zealand, the Caribbean and England, as well as more than one former Test player from each country. For me this match has become the annual setting for a marvellous five-day reunion with international cricketers of different vintages.

On this occasion I had two worries. First, could England, after losing by an innings and plenty at Edgbaston, bounce back and provide Clive Lloyd and company with a reasonable contest? I was not too hopeful because our attack, arguably the worst we have fielded in this country since the war, was insipid and there was also a big question mark against our batting line-up. If this sounds harsh, let us examine the make-up of the England XI. Bob Willis had been an outstanding fast bowler, but was retiring at the end of the season. His haul at the time was 8 wickets at 47.25 each and, though still effective in limited-overs cricket, there was doubt as to his ability to come back for a third and fourth spell. Ian Botham had been well below his best as a bowler for the past two years and Miller's record with the ball was undistinguished. The two Essex representatives, Derek Pringle and novice Neil Foster, were not in the same class as their county colleague, the banned John Lever, yet John himself had never been an international regular.

Our batting cannot be said to have inspired too much confidence. Of the three genuine Test-class players, Gower looked bowed down with the cares of captaincy, Lamb had been without runs in Test cricket for too long and Botham has never been reliable. Of the others, Fowler had been painfully uncomfortable in the First Test, Broad had been picked on the not too convincing evidence of having made runs in county cricket when the standard of the non overseas bowling was very low, and Gatting, despite unquestionable ability and numerous opportunities, had failed to score at the highest level. In sharp contrast the West Indies were an experienced and extremely able side. Although the omens were not good, for four days England more than held their own, only to blow up on the fifth when Greenidge and Gomes were permitted to romp home by 9 wickets with plenty of overs to spare.

My second worry was whether I possessed sufficient stamina to last five days, always assuming the game lasted that long. In addition to my duties with TMS, which entailed consuming vast quantities of 'Johnstonian goodies', writing, driving up and back to Westcliff each day and meeting a host of cricketing friends (many of whom I had not seen since the 1983 Lord's Test), there was also the menace of the Lord's boxes, to say nothing of the Arbours. One can be innocently walking round the ground when a figure and a voice you know too well cajoles you inside a well-furbished box. There the hospitality will be exceptional. The problem lies in escaping!

I had gone to collect a letter from my car one lunchtime and was making my way back to the commentary box via the Arbour where the Cricketers' Club as usual were lunching. Without too much difficulty, the 'Gaffer' Frank Russell persuaded me to accept a glass of wine while I talked to two people, one I had last seen in Barbados, the other in Australia. It was a pleasant interlude and I continued on my way, but considerable stealth was required to avoid two boxes, further delays, and a distinguished former player who was already well gone and looking for a violent, pointless argument.

I was also committed to four social functions starting, on the Tuesday before the Test, with practice at Bedford College, which consisted of speaking and helping to award colours to the undergraduates. My second net was a Lord's Taverners Dinner at the Café Royal on the eve of the Test. This was held to honour that distinguished 50-year-old partnership between the Middlesex twins, Denis Compton and Bill Edrich. As I found myself on the same table as Denis, Bill, Keith Miller, Terry Wogan, the two speakers, Barry Cryer and Frank Crozier, and John Bromley, the Taverners' new President, it was a fairly chatty evening when quite a few fancy shots, or shots of fancy, were played.

The next morning I left my home in Westcliff with plenty of time to reach Lord's. Although employing all the back-doubles, which took me past such varied and intriguing landmarks as Chigwell School, Holloway Prison, Arsenal Football Ground, Hilldrop Crescent, (where Crippen murdered his wife) and Bill Frindall's favourite taverna, as well as through one almost

entirely Caribbean precinct and another district largely populated by Orthodox Jews, my journey took two and a quarter hours, instead of the intended one hour and 20 minutes.

The match was held up during the morning because of the weather, and I chatted with Reg Simpson, whom I had once seen make a big 100 in Sydney on a fast pitch when the three fast bowlers had provided a constant barrage of bouncers, usually two per over. He had not been hit and had not hooked. His technique was to move back and across and then sway inside, or outside, the line of the ball. I also had a talk with Godfrey Evans, who was providing the odds on the game. He was much impressed by both the 'keeping, and the sensible batting, of Downton, who was to be one of England's few real successes of the summer.

Thursday, shortened by bad weather and bad light, belonged very much to England, after they had been put in on a wicket which was rather slower than expected. At lunch, the new opening partnership were still together with 46 runs on the board and at tea they had taken the score to the prosperity of three figures without loss. In his first Test, Broad made a good 55 while Fowler, who had been in some danger of losing his place, scored a brave, if somewhat improbable, century. When stumps were drawn we were 167 for 2 and I went contentedly to meet my wife at the Royal Garden where we were attending an international Dinner hosted by Omnisport, for whom I am a consultant. In the course of an enjoyable evening, I was able to tell Ken Rosewall that I was the only man in the room to have seen him play with Lew Hoad in the Davis Cup against Seixas and Trabert in Sydney.

After the delays of the previous day, I decided to use the Walthamstow route, but the improvement was minimal. At Lord's I ran into, not literally, a couple of useful hookers, Everton Weekes and Colin Milburn. Neither had ever been hit on the head, but they had not made the mistake of taking their eyes off the ball.

From the comparative prosperity of 167 for 2 England stumbled to 248 for 6 at lunch and were all out for 286, with Marshall, 6 for 84, the main executioner. Home team disappointment was largely quelled by 2 early Botham wickets, but more important was the way Ian was running in with a zest and bounce which had been absent from his bowling for some time. He was also swinging the ball in the air. At close of play, the West Indies were 119 for 3 with Vivian Richards at the crease, so that the game was wide open, and everything pointed to a fascinating Saturday. I made my way to Brian Johnston's home, situated appropriately enough in Boundary Road, where Brian holds court every year during the Lord's Test, while Pauline, his wife, does the important things like producing the food and the drink, both excellent. The Johnston party is invariably held in the garden, and in beautiful weather, confirming my belief that Brian really does know everybody worth knowing, including the Almighty.

As usual at the weekend there were no problems driving up to Lord's, but the West Indies found plenty when they were batting, especially from a rejuvenated Botham, who returned the magnificent figures of 8 for 103. He was well supported by Willis who was unlucky not to finish with a bigger haul. At lunch the West Indies had scraped to 213 for 6, though an umpiring error was responsible for the loss of Richards, and were all out shortly after 2.30 for 245, giving England a most gratifying and unexpected lead.

Botham bowled unchanged from 11.00 am; in fact it was difficult to see how anybody could have taken the ball from him. I have never seen a bowler, apart from Fred Trueman, grab the ball and remove his sweater quicker at the end of each over from the other end. However, well as he bowled, I have a feeling his figures, in terms of runs conceded, would have been even better if he had had a short rest. It also seemed rather strange that Foster should be confined to only 6 overs, whereas Pringle was entrusted with 11, distinctly expensive ones.

England started badly, losing Broad for 0, but reached 114 for 4 at close. Saturday had been a good day, the sun had shone, Botham's bowling had been back to its ebullient best, and England had led on the first innings to show that the West Indies were not quite as formidable as was sometimes imagined. I had lunch with the TCCB but the most happy feature for me was the number of smiling faces among former England players. These included David Allen, Fred Trueman, Denis Compton, Mike Smith, Len Hutton and Doug Insole. We naturally do not like to see England lose, but we *hate* seeing England being humiliated, which happened so frequently last summer and that hurt.

During the day I encountered Keith Miller and Dennis Atkinson, a couple of handy all-rounders. Both, however, are convinced that their expertise with the horses far exceeds their former skill with bat and ball, a view with which I do not concur. To me, their respective bookmakers look a shade too affluent, as they step from the 'family runabout', a 1984 Roller.

On the Monday I decided to try yet another route to the ground, which included spells on the M11 and M25, before turning off at the South Mimms Roundabout, and which is possibly quicker, providing that, unlike me, one knows the way to Lord's from the A1. The pitch by now was placid and for once the West Indian attack looked comparatively innocuous. After lunch Lamb and Botham enjoyed an exhilarating partnership and at tea with 226 for 5, England were, if not in a winning position, at least in a stronger one than the tourists. At this stage, although a draw seemed the most probable outcome, an England victory was certainly feasible.

In the final session Botham departed for an impressive 81 and, with the score 287 for 7, Lamb not out 109, even the formidable Garner posed few threats. Then with England wanting as many runs, and as much time as possible, if they were to have any chance of winning the match, Lamb and Pringle decided to go off for bad light. This was an incomprehensible decision which both delighted and amazed the West Indian players, who for the only time in the series had lost the initiative and were struggling. Quite apart from the other considerations, it is easier to score runs against a tired,

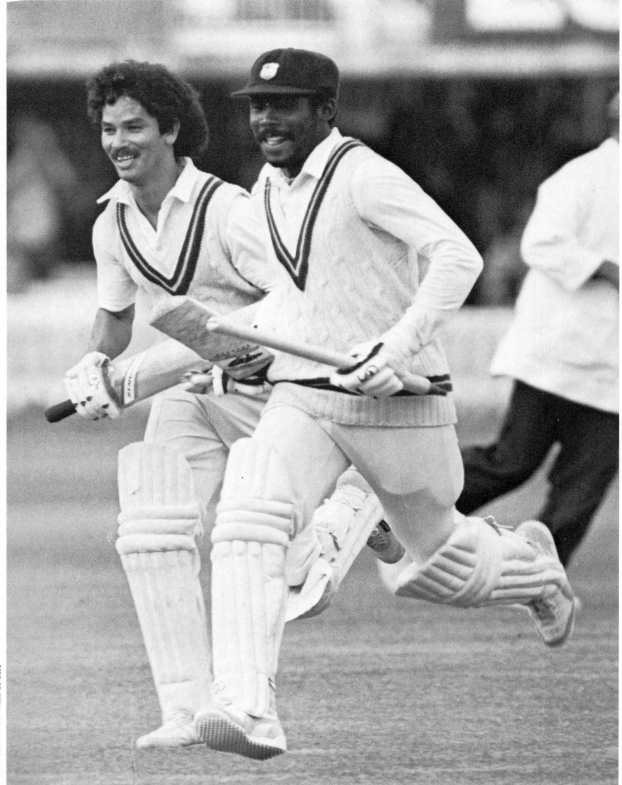

and somewhat dispirited attack in the evening when one batsman already has a hundred in the bank, than on the next morning, when the bowlers are fresh and the batsmen have to settle in again.

On the final day I reverted to my normal route and no traffic problems occurred, but I was totally unprepared for what occurred out in the middle. I thought an England victory improbable, since, if we could score over 300 runs against the tourists' bowling, it was unlikely that our much weaker attack would dismiss the West Indies in the time available. Our best chance, I felt, lay in the visitors getting within sight of their target, as wickets are always liable to fall when chasing runs against the clock. However, the most likely result was clearly a draw and I never even considered a West Indian victory.

The day started with England using up time and losing some wickets as they moved to a declaration of 300 for 9, which was intended to be too many for the opposition to reach in the time available. But perhaps a miracle would happen and wickets start tumbling. A miracle happened, but not the one England wanted.

The West Indies began their second innings thoughtfully, yet despite Haynes being run out for 17 they had reached 82 for 1 at lunch. This was due more to poor bowling and over-attacking fields than to any positive action by the batsmen. The morning frolic turned into a post-lunch gallop as Greenidge and Gomes, in the afternoon session, took the total to 214, and turned the last period into a formality. The West Indies finished up 344 for 1, winning by 9 wickets, with 9 overs of the final 20 unrequired!

The batting of Greenidge was brilliant, Gomes provided the ideal support but Gower remained on the offensive for too long. A third man after the opening spell would conservatively have saved around 40 runs. Although he failed to recognise the danger early enough, he was also handicapped by some of the worst bowling it has ever been my misfortune to see at international level. With the exception of Willis, nobody seemed capable of maintaining anything even approaching a reasonable line or length, or bowling to their field. It was hard to understand why Botham from round the wicket with an off-side field appeared to be attacking Gomes' leg-stump.

Driving back after that impossible victory, I felt sad that England, who had played above themselves for most of the contest, should then have thrown it all away on that final day. It made assessing the strength of this fine West Indian team even harder, because our attack was well below Test standards, our batting was unexceptional and on black Tuesday evening our fielding disintegrated.

We did it! Larry Gomes and Gordon Greenidge leave the field after the epic win at Lord's.

ENGLAND 1st INNINGS v. WEST INDIES (2nd TEST) AT LORD'S, LONDON ON 28,29,30 JUNE, 2,3 JULY, 1984.

TOSS: WEST INDIES

IN	OUT	MINS	No.	BATSMAN	HOW OUT	BOWLER	RUNS	WKT	TOTAL	6s	4s	BALLS	NOTES ON DISMISSAL
11.03	12.45	366	1	G. FOWLER	C' HARPER	BAPTISTE	106	5	243	.	13	259	HS in TESTS (2nd) Edged drive to 2nd slip
11.03	5.00	156	2	B.C. BROAD	C' DUJON	MARSHALL	55	1	101	.	9	115	Leg-glanced short ball – excellent leg-side catch
5.02	5.14	12	3	D.I. GOWER*	LBW	MARSHALL	3	2	106	.	.	9	Played back – beaten by pace – breakback
5.16	11.20	109	4	A.J. LAMB	LBW	MARSHALL	23	3	183	.	3	77	Played back – fast ball kept low
11.22	11.30	8	5	M.W. GATTING	LBW	MARSHALL	1	4	185	.	.	7	Padded up to ball on off stump
11.33	12.58	85	6	I.T. BOTHAM	C' RICHARDS	BAPTISTE	30	6	248	.	4	66	Square gully – ball 'popped' – off shoulder of bat
12.48	(3.10)	97	7	P.R. DOWNTON†	NOT OUT		23			.	3	62	
1.43	1.54	11	8	G. MILLER	RUN OUT (BAPTISTE)		0	7	251	.	.	6	Beaten by astonishing throw from deep fine leg – bowler's end middle stump
1.56	2.15	19	9	D.R. PRINGLE	LBW	GARNER	2	8	255	.	.	13	Padded up to break back that would have hit middle & off
2.17	2.41	24	10	N.A. FOSTER	C' HARPER	MARSHALL	6	9	264	.	.	24	Edged push to 3rd slip
2.43	3.10	27	11	R.G.D. WILLIS	BOWLED	MARSHALL	2	10	286	.	.	14	Late on stroke
				* CAPTAIN † WICKET-KEEPER		EXTRAS	b 4 lb 14 w 2 nb 15			35			

TOTAL (105.5 OVERS ; 466 MINUTES) 286 all out at 3.10pm on second day.   0s 32 4s 652 balls (including 17 no balls)

13 OVERS 4 BALLS/HOUR
2.70 RUNS/OVER
44 RUNS/100 BALLS

BOWLER	O	M	R	W	nb w		HRS	OVERS	RUNS
GARNER	32	10	67	1	3/-		1	15	44
SMALL	9	0	38	0			2	13	42
MARSHALL	36.5	10	85	6	9/2		3	13	20
BAPTISTE	20	6	36	2	4/4		4	14	46
HARPER	8	0	25	0	2/-		5	14	35
			35	1			6	14	52
	105.5	26	286	10			7	13	17

2ND NEW BALL taken at 2.10pm 2nd day.
ENGLAND 253-7 after 93.1 overs.

RUNS	MINS	OVERS	LAST 50 (in mins)
50	69	17.2	69
100	147	35.0	78
150	233	54.0	86
200	316	73.0	83
250	388	89.3	72

LUNCH: 46-0 [16 OVERS FOWLER 11*] [63 MIN. BROAD 29*]
BAD LIGHT & RAIN STOPPED PLAY 11.55 TO 12.50 PM (55 MIN. LOST)

TEA: 100-0 [36 OVERS FOWLER 30*] [151 MIN. BROAD 54*]
BAD LIGHT & RAIN STOPPED PLAY 3.35 TO 3.37 PM (62 MIN. LOST)

STUMPS: 167-2 [61 OVERS FOWLER 70* (3d)] [262 MIN. LAMB 13* (5b)]
1ST DAY – NETT TIME LOST: 96 MIN.

LUNCH: 248-6 [87 OVERS 379 MINUTES] [DOWNTON 0* (10 MIN)]

MARSHALL TOOK FIVE WICKETS IN A TEST INNINGS FOR THE SIXTH TIME (FIFTH IN LAST EIGHT MATCHES).

WKT	PARTNERSHIP		RUNS	MINS
1st	Fowler	Broad	101	156
2nd	Fowler	Gower	5	12
3rd	Fowler	Lamb	77	109
4th	Fowler	Gatting	2	8
5th	Fowler	Botham	58	73
6th	Botham	Downton	5	10
7th	Downton	Miller	3	11
8th	Downton	Pringle	4	19
9th	Downton	Foster	9	24
10th	Downton	Willis	22	27
			286	

Compiled by BILL FRINDALL

WEST INDIES 1st INNINGS

IN REPLY TO ENGLAND'S 286 ALL OUT

IN	OUT	MINS	No.	BATSMAN	HOW OUT	BOWLER	RUNS	WKT	TOTAL	6s	4s	BALLS	NOTES ON DISMISSAL
3.24	3.29	5	1	C.G. GREENIDGE	C' MILLER	BOTHAM	1	1	1	.	.	7	Edged outswinger low to 2nd slip – superb falling catch
3.24	3.42	18	2	D.L. HAYNES	LBW	BOTHAM	12	2	18	.	2	12	Played back – hit on back leg by breakback
3.31	4.25	35	3	H.A. GOMES	C' GATTING	BOTHAM	10	3	35	.	2	24	Edged via pad to forward short leg – dived forward (right-hand ct.)
4.01	11.33	153	4	I.V.A. RICHARDS	C' GATTING	BOTHAM	72	4	138	.	11	94	Beaten by breakback
4.27	12.24	178	5	C.H. LLOYD*	LBW	BOTHAM	39	6	173	.	5	129	7th to 7000 RUNS when 25. Added 7 of 59 balls on 3rd morning
11.35	11.46	11	6	P.J. DUJON†	C' FOWLER	BOTHAM	8	5	147	.	1	8	Top-edged hook – skier to mid-wicket
11.48	1.43	75	7	M.D. MARSHALL	C' PRINGLE	WILLIS	29	7	213	1	4	39	Edged lifting ball to 1st slip
12.26	2.25	79	8	E.A.E. BAPTISTE	C' DOWNTON	WILLIS	44	9	241	.	7	56	Edged low to keeper's right
1.45	2.01	16	9	R.A. HARPER	C' GATTING	BOTHAM	8	8	231	.	1	12	Drove half-volley low to cover
2.03	2.32	29	10	J. GARNER	C' DOWNTON	BOTHAM	6	10	245	.	.	19	Edged low to keeper's right
2.27	(2.32)	5	11	M.A. SMALL	NOT OUT		3			.	.	3	First innings in Tests
				* CAPTAIN † WICKET-KEEPER		EXTRAS	b – lb 5 w 1 nb 7			13			

TOTAL (65.4 OVERS ; 310 MINUTES) 245 ALL OUT at 2.32pm on third day.   1s 33 4s 403 balls (including 9 no balls)

ENGLAND'S LEAD : 41 RUNS

12 OVERS 4 BALLS/HOUR
3.73 RUNS/OVER
61 RUNS/100 BALLS

BOWLER	O	M	R	W	nb w		HRS	OVERS	RUNS
WILLIS	19	5	48	2	4/-		1	12	41
BOTHAM	27.4	6	103	8	-/1		2	13	59
PRINGLE	11	0	54	0	5/-		3	14	43
FOSTER	6	2	13	0			4	12	46
MILLER	2	0	14	0	.		5	13	52
			13						
	65.4	13	245	10					

RUNS	MINS	OVERS	LAST 50 (in mins)
50	75	15.4	75
100	119	24.5	44
150	194	41.3	75
200	244	51.5	50

TEA: 18-2 [GOMES 5* (11 minutes)] [4 OVERS. 18 MINUTES.]

STUMPS: 119-3 [30 OVERS RICHARDS 6* (121)] [139 MIN LLOYD 32* (95)]
(2ND DAY) 167 BEHIND

LUNCH: 213-6 [56 OVERS MARSHALL 29* (74)] [260 MIN BAPTISTE 32* (36)]
73 BEHIND

WKT	PARTNERSHIP		RUNS	MINS
1st	Greenidge	Haynes	1	5
2nd	Haynes	Gomes	17	18
3rd	Gomes	Richards	17	24
4th	Richards	Lloyd	103	127
5th	Lloyd	Dujon	9	11
6th	Lloyd	Marshall	26	36
7th	Marshall	Baptiste	40	37
8th	Baptiste	Harper	18	16
9th	Baptiste	Garner	10	22
10th	Garner	Small	4	5
			245	

Compiled by BILL FRINDALL

ENGLAND 2ND INNINGS — 41 RUNS AHEAD ON FIRST INNINGS

IN	OUT	MINS	No.	BATSMAN	HOW OUT	BOWLER	RUNS	WKT	TOTAL	6s	4s	BALLS	NOTES ON DISMISSAL
2.44	4.21	76	1	G. FOWLER	LBW	SMALL	11	3	36		2	53	Played back to ball that moved back sharply
2.44	2.53	9	2	B.C. BROAD	C' HARPER	GARNER	0	1	5	·	·	3	Edged ball that lifted and left him to 3rd slip
2.55	4.18	62	3	D.I. GOWER *	C' LLOYD	SMALL	21	2	33		2	42	Edged off-drive low to 1st slip - ball 'left' him
4.20	11.10	360	4	A.J. LAMB	C' DUJON	MARSHALL	110	8	290		13	259	4th in Tests. Edged drive.
4.23	5.33	70	5	M.W. GATTING	LBW	MARSHALL	29	4	88	·	4	49	Padded up to straight ball for second time in match
5.36	3.56	165	6	I.T. BOTHAM	LBW	GARNER	81	5	216	1	9	111	(4000 runs when 62) 50 off 40 balls. Pushed forward - misjudged line
3.58	4.43	25	7	P.R. DOWNTON†	LBW	SMALL	4	6	230	·	·	20	Yorked on foot by late inswinger
4.45	5.41	56	8	G. MILLER	BOWLED	HARPER	9	7	273	·	1	33	Beaten by off-spin - off stump hit
5.43	11.19	40	9	D.R. PRINGLE	LBW	GARNER	8	9	300	·	1	26	Played back - beaten by breakback. 12th LBW - Test Match Record
11.13	(11.19)	6	10	N.A. FOSTER	NOT OUT		9			·	2	4	
			11	R.G.D. WILLIS	DID NOT BAT								

* CAPTAIN   † WICKET-KEEPER

EXTRAS b 4 lb 7 w 1 nb 6   **18**   1st 34s 600 balls (including 9 no balls)

TOTAL (98.3 OVERS, 443 MINUTES) **300 - 9** DECLARED at 11.19 am on fifth day.

13 OVERS 2 BALLS/HOUR
3.05 RUNS/OVER
50 RUNS/100 BALLS

(SETTING WEST INDIES 342 TO WIN IN 270 MINUTES PLUS 20 OVERS)

BOWLER	O	M	R	W	nb/w	HRS	OVERS	RUNS
GARNER	30.3	3	91	3	7/-	1	13	21
MARSHALL	22	6	85	2	7/1	2	13	49
SMALL	12	2	40	3	·	3	13	53
BAPTISTE	26	8	48	0	·	4	12	59
HARPER	8	1	18	1	·	5	14	28
			18			6	14	23
	98.3	20	300	9		7	14	50

RUNS	MINS	OVERS	LAST 50 (in mins)
50	91	19.3	91
100	162	35.3	71
150	208	45.0	46
200	277	59.5	69
250	375	83.5	98
300	440	98.0	65

TEA: 20-1 [12 OVERS 56 MIN.] FOWLER 6* (56 min) GOWER 13* (45 min)

STUMPS: 114-4 (3rd DAY) (155 AHEAD) 38 OVERS; 175 MIN LAMB 30* (100 min) BOTHAM 17* (24 min)

LUNCH: 144-4 AT 12.46 (185 AHEAD) 43.5 OVERS; 205 MIN 115 MIN LOST. R.S.P. 11.30 - 2.15 LAMB 44* (161) BOTHAM 32* (54')

TEA: 226-5 (267 AHEAD) [73 OVERS 331 MIN] LAMB 72* (256 min) DOWNTON 1* (13 min)

STUMPS: 287-7 (328 AHEAD) [95 OVERS 426 MIN] 109'LOST (NET) LAMB 109* (351 min) PRINGLE 6* (23 min)

WKT	PARTNERSHIP		RUNS	MINS
1st	Fowler	Broad	5	9
2nd	Fowler	Gower	28	62
3rd	Fowler	Lamb	3	1
4th	Lamb	Gatting	52	70
5th	Lamb	Botham	128	165
6th	Lamb	Downton	14	25
7th	Lamb	Miller	43	56
8th	Lamb	Pringle	17	32
9th	Pringle	Foster	10	6
10th			(300)	

Compiled by BILL FRINDALL

WEST INDIES 2ND INNINGS — SET TO SCORE 342 RUNS IN A MINIMUM OF 328 MINUTES

IN	OUT	MINS	No.	BATSMAN	HOW OUT	BOWLER	RUNS	WKT	TOTAL	6s	4s	BALLS	NOTES ON DISMISSAL
11.32	(5.31)	300	1	C.G. GREENIDGE	NOT OUT		214			2	29	241	HS in Tests
11.32	12.34	62	2	D.L. HAYNES	RUN OUT (LAMB)		17	1	57	·	2	29	Attempted run to backward square-leg - sent back - slipped
12.36	(5.31)	236	3	H.A. GOMES	NOT OUT		92			·	13	140	
			4	I.V.A. RICHARDS									
			5	C.H. LLOYD*									
			6	P.J. DUJON†									
			7	M.D. MARSHALL	Did not bat								
			8	E.A.E. BAPTISTE									
			9	R.A. HARPER									
			10	J. GARNER									
			11	M.A. SMALL									

* CAPTAIN   † WICKET-KEEPER

EXTRAS b 4 lb 4 w - nb 13   **21**   2nd 44s 410 balls (including 13 no balls)

TOTAL (66.1 OVERS, 300 MINUTES) **344 - 1**

13 OVERS 1 BALLS/HOUR
5.12 RUNS/OVER
84 RUNS/100 BALLS

BOWLER	O	M	R	W	nb	HRS	OVERS	RUNS
WILLIS	15	5	48	0	9	1	14	57
BOTHAM	20.1	2	117	0	·	2	13	53
PRINGLE	8	0	44	0	4	3	12	80
FOSTER	12	0	69	0	·	4	13	66
MILLER	11	0	45	0	·	5	14	84
			21					
	66.1	7	344	0				

RUNS	MINS	OVERS	LAST 50 (in mins)
50	54	12.3	54
100	112	25.0	58
150	149	33.1	37
200	199	42.3	50
250	231	49.4	32
300	271	58.4	40

LUNCH: 82-1 [20 OVERS 90 MIN] GREENIDGE 54* (76') GOMES 4* (24')

TEA: 214-1 [45 OVERS 210 MIN.] GREENIDGE 125* (210) GOMES 52* (146')

WEST INDIES WON BY NINE WICKETS WITH 11.5 OVERS TO SPARE

MEN OF THE MATCH: I.T. BOTHAM and (FIRST JOINT AWARD) C.G. GREENIDGE

Adjudicator: T.G. EVANS

TOTAL TIME LOST: 3 HOURS 25 MIN (NET)

WKT	PARTNERSHIP		RUNS	MINS
1st	Greenidge	Haynes	57	62
2nd	Greenidge	Gomes	287*	236
			344	

Compiled by BILL FRINDALL

FROM OUR CORRESPONDENTS
Peter Baxter

No household chores by me are done
When there's a Test Match to be won,
(Or lost, of course – it makes no odds
If we win or the other bods).
The skills presented just the same
All part of this exciting game.

In comfort, then, and at a glance
I watch the pageantry advance
In silence – for I much prefer
To hear those voices from the air.
Johnners, Boil, Blowers and the rest
Perform with gaiety and zest.

With testimonials like that, from Helen Ottaway-Wilson in South Croydon, can you wonder that we enjoy opening our post-bag, even though at times we are snowed under by it. The letters all get read and eventually – in some way – I hope they all get answered. One correspondent in 1984 – Trevor Littlechild of Cambridge – showed less than total devotion to the commentary, though, when he suggested that the way to take opposition wickets was to switch off his radio and go out to mow the lawn, on the not very sound theory that the most exciting things happen when you are not listening! It may sound strange, but such superstitions exist in most English first-class dressing-rooms. I have seen England players during a Test Match who will not change their seats if a promising partnership is building.

Paul and Bridget Brooks of Buxted in Sussex have become so influenced by TMS that they named their two new kittens 'Johnners' and 'Blowers'. Unfortunately the vet revealed soon afterwards that the two were females! Paul and Bridget enclosed a photograph of Blowers tweaking Johnners' tail (the kittens, that is).

The enigmatic 'Tommy T.' of Orpington was disturbed to hear one of the team say, 'Trevor opens the window and Botham is in ...' I think even Ian uses the door – most of the time. These sort of letters are generally addressed to Brian – many of them not remotely to do with cricket, as was the case with Peter Foley who wrote from Seven Kings in Essex with a sign he had observed, 'Take Away Chinese Food' underneath which had been scrawled, 'And bring back Bangers and Mash'. And from nearby Hoddesdon Roy Griggs posed an off-beat quiz question: 'What is the maximum number of people allowed on to a cricket field during a match, and how many wickets would be down at the time?' The answer – 18. That's 11 fielders, 2 batsmen, both with runners, 2 umpires and the groundsman asking the fielding captain for his choice of roller because 9 wickets are down.

Jack Armstrong wrote from Oakdale near Poole with a question which seemed to be aimed at me. Why can cricket followers in places like Australia, the West Indies and India follow live commentary through the night while we in England do not usually have the same facilities? The answer is, as with most things, economic. There is no point in our hiring expensive satellite circuit time and opening transmitters if there are more people alive in Broadcasting House for the commentary than there are listening at home. On the whole the playing hours in England suit our opposite numbers better than theirs do us. For instance, even in the Eastern states of Australia a Test Match in England starts at 8 pm while for us at home a Test Match at Melbourne or Sydney starts at midnight. We have steadily increased our live relays of overseas Tests over the last eight years or so and on the last two Australian tours have broadcast from midnight to 2.00 am and from 5.00 to 7.00 am – the close of play. To return to the economic factor, the other countries can pick up the commentary from the World Service, while those who have a similar service are not beaming it at us.

In 1984, as in a few other years, there was a great deal of complaint about the noise from the crowd of can-banging, horns and whistles. People wrote asking why we had to place microphones in the middle of the crowd. We did not, of course. Most of the noise was just what was coming through the window, which was as wearing for us as it was for the listener. It also made it very difficult to hear now much was being transmitted. We did try various ways of reducing the noise, but, ironically, for the Test where we have our only totally enclosed box – Headingley (where Fred's pipe, for that reason, created a vision problem as well) – we had a large number of complaints about the lack of atmosphere. You just can't win! Funnily enough, at Headingley (even without Fred's pipe) we all felt very cut off. There were other times, though, when the cacophony became almost melodic and I do recall Don Mosey appreciating the rhythm at Old Trafford, which prompted a spoof (I think) letter from a gentleman named Bongo Wells, who addressed himself to F. S. Trueman: 'How come you don't like the Caribbean beat, man? We don't know why you keep coming on so heavy 'bout the brothers hitting the steel. All the brothers here get good vibes from Sir Don Mosey, cos he's where it's at! He raps along with the beat. Even old Henry Blofeld ain't as much of a dude as he sounds. Reckon he's pretty laid back cos he lets the sound flow over him. We like Mr Johnston cos he tells it like it is even when it isn't, dig?' We suspected the hand of that often-disguised letter-writer, Peter Richardson!

The awesome power of the West Indies as they swept inexorably

towards their 5-0 whitewash provoked plenty of suggestions as to how England's cricket could be improved or the opposition handicapped. Geoff Cox of Harpenden was not alone in highlighting the way that English county experience had helped the West Indies. He pointed out that Jeff Dujon's 100 at Old Trafford was the first by one of this team without that experience and there were suggestions that no overseas player in county cricket should be included in a touring team. A rare correspondent from the USA, Jim Babb, suggested a separate international team for the county championship to provide Test-class opposition as a matter of course for all county players and thus improve standards.

While England suffered the onslaught, Simon Louison wrote from New Zealand to remind us of his country's record against the West Indies over the last 28 years in which time they have not lost a series to them. It might have been pointed out that they had not played a great deal — partly because of New Zealand rugby links with South Africa. Six-year-old David Stanhope said, 'When I play cricket with my Dad, I let him win so he feels happy sometimes. Why don't the West Indies let England win so they feel better?' A good thought. And Derek Allan thought that the headline writers had missed a trick by not using his line: 'Greenidge gives England Mean Time'.

A great deal was said both in the letters and indeed on the air on the subject of the South African bans. The unavailability of Gooch and Emburey for England was naturally to the fore and rather less was made of the West Indies loss of such as Sylvester Clarke, but the results showed that to be apparently less of a blow. Eileen Mewes, writing from an address near enough to Lord's, praised the Sri Lankan manager, Neil Chanmugam, for belittling the effect of the banning of his own country's South African 'rebels'.

A recent worrying phenomenon more immediately related to the playing of the game has been the habit of crowds rushing on as the last ball of a match — particularly a one-day game — is bowled. Tony Mason from Cornwall voiced the concern of many when he questioned how anyone could know what the final margin of victory could be when the ball is so often lost in a charging horde and a winning run is frequently not actually completed. In tight finishes this could become a major problem, but heaven forbid that we should ever see the crowd fenced in as in the large football grounds.

We always get a number of letters from parents whose children attend schools at which there are no facilities for learning or playing cricket. The former Kent and England player, Bob Woolmer, who, sadly, was forced by injury during 1984 to announce his retirement, wrote to tell us of a helpful video-cassette which he and Alan Knott had put together for anybody teaching 8- to 12-year-olds. He offered more information to anyone writing to him at Kent. Blind listeners are also always keen to gain more information on the game and early in the season we were asked by one to relate field placings to the numbers on a clock face. This prompted another blind listener to offer to produce this as a braille aid, and the RNIB were quick to volunteer it as a service to anyone who would write to them in Great Portland Street, London W1.

Much of our mail presses the claims of local heroes to an England place. 1984 was remarkable for the falling off in correspondence from Hampshire supporting Trevor Jesty, which had persisted for years. He, it seemed, had lost favour there to Mark Nicholas. (We are often assumed if not to be all on the selection committee, then at least to form the selectors' opinions for them!) Many letters came from Lancashire at any suggestion that Graeme Fowler was not thoroughly on top of the West Indian attack and Derek Randall, who lost his place after having to bat unhappily at number three in the First Test, had plenty of support from Nottinghamshire. Keith Edwards wrote from Swansea to press the claim of Glamorgan's emerging fast bowler, Greg Thomas, and was one of many who raised the old chestnut of 'unfashionable counties'.

While we hear of these younger players, many of our older listeners write with memories of past heroes. John Lerner of Harrow landed in Sicily in 1943 with Hedley Verity, who was killed later in that campaign, and he recalled the great man demonstrating his spinning grip on an orange as the ship approached the theatre of war. Bill Voce died during the 1984 season and Norman Mulvey was prompted by this sad news to write from Chester recalling a match at Trent Bridge when the left-arm pace-bowler took 8 Australian wickets in the tour match against the county in 1934. This was soon enough after the infamous 'Bodyline' series and this time Voce was bowling without the support of his Nottinghamshire partner, Harold Larwood. In the Lord's Test against the West Indies an MCC Young Cricketer, Don Topley, fielding as twelfth man for England took a splendid catch on the boundary, only to put a foot over the rope and see a 6 signalled. This prompted memories of 'Copley's catch' from Janet Wilson of Sheffield. He, too, was fielding substitute for England – this time against Australia at Trent Bridge in 1930. S. H. Copley caught Stan McCabe at wide mid-on when he and Bradman looked like winning a match which eventually went to England by 93 runs. Janet Wilson had learnt the story at the knee of her father, who witnessed the deed, and it became Copley's finest hour, for he never made the grade in first-class cricket.

We have already had a sample of the verse TMS receives, and Patrick Scott of Haslingden (a place not unknown to Clive Lloyd) offered this apposite contribution:

When I was young they used to say:
'You try too hard to bowl too fast.
The pace may come; perhaps it won't,
But accuracy will always pay.
First get them straight and bowl a length.
When you can put them where you want
And hit a spot four out of six,
Then is the time to speed them up
And if you can't get Larwood pace,
At least you will make batsmen play
And get some out'. And so one did.

When I was young they also said:
'For heaven's sake don't bowl long-hops'.
But nowadays long-hops are praised.
Bouncers they call them now, of course.

And something of that was taken up by Valerie Robertson of St Albans.

Oh, how I used to love cricket.
It made summer richer for me.
   The courteous crowd;
   Few bouncers allowed;
Such elegant chivalry.

When will we ever see cricket
As it was intended to be?
   A chance to see strokes
   From confident blokes
Who know they will live to take tea.

After a five-Test battering at the hands of the fast bowlers we received a flood of correspondence appreciating the quality of the Sri Lankan play that followed it. So many people seemed to enjoy the old-fashioned virtues that one was forced to wonder if modern-day promoters of 'blood-and-guts' cricket – particularly in Australia – have got it right.

There are always those who suggest changes to the laws of the game itself. The injuries which put Andy Lloyd and Paul Terry out of matches probably prompted the suggestions of teams of 12 or 13 from which only 11 could field at any one time and only 11 bat in the same innings. The structure of English county cricket, too, always comes in for its fair share of alternative proposals, 16 four-day matches being a great favourite, though some would like the inclusion of an eighteenth county. In the meantime the poor facilities at some county grounds are bemoaned by such as Mrs Grace Mason of Grays in Essex, one of the counties whose facilities – at Chelmsford, at least – have improved beyond all recognition in the last ten years. It is true, though, that in these days of rival entertainments families have got to be made more welcome if the crowds are to be attracted. An irritation for Christopher Dean (who says he does not skate with Jayne Torvill) is the persistent hold-up for moving behind the bowler's arm and he suggested one-way glass sight-screens to prevent this. A less expensive solution might be a wider version of the lattice-work screens favoured in Australia, which have spectators seated behind them. Paul Hooper had photographic evidence to support the claim that this is a particular problem at Headingley Tests with a shot of two sleeping stewards there.

1984 was the year that Italy became an affiliated member of the International Cricket Conference. If this need not yet cause great fluttering in the dovecotes of Test-playing countries it has, as one Ruggiero Vilchi pointed out, given us some colourful new expressions. The bowler is known as *lanciatore* but the batsman does not get away so lightly. He is *chi batte la palla*, although I think Italian TMS commentators might be allowed to call him the *colpitore*. And an umpire would have to think long and hard before giving someone run out: '*Metter fuori dal gioco il coliptore chi cerca fare un corso.*' 'How's that' is at least concise: '*Com'era!*'

Another foreign language was invoked by John Hollis from Llanidloes who asked if two players with the same name in different languages had ever played in the same Test side before. His pair in question were Lamb and Agnew, Agnew's name being derived from the French *agneau*.

It is no secret that we receive a great number of good things to eat. We are always very grateful, although I have noticed with some slight alarm that occasionally a generous gift is not an entirely altruistic gesture when a firm's name is presented as the donor. However we were very interested to receive some national delicacies from the Sinhala Association of Sri Lankans in the UK, in the form of Kokis – a sort of potato crisp in butterfly shapes – and Arak – a fiendish spirit made from coconut flower.

Many a family has invented games to keep the children amused in the car on a long journey and 11-year-old Jonathan Taylor offered his family's favourite: Motorway Cricket. The colours of cars overtaking or overtaken provide the scoring:

A Blue car scores one run	Purple: five
Yellow: two	Brown: six
Green: three	Other colours: no run
Red: four	White: a wicket

A cream car, says Jonathan, is worth an appeal, with the driver as umpire. He also adds, for Henry Blofeld's benefit, that on English roads an auto-rickshaw scores ten!

Finally back to our poets. Edward Cast offered us a series of limericks. Here are three:

> An aggressive young batter called Botham,
> Being ragged by his mates thought he'd showtham.
>   With one mighty six
>   He demolished the bricks
> And supports of the pav. just belowtham.

> A new-minted skipper called Gower
> Was expected to burst into flower.
>   But a dicey decision
>   Not to bat in poor vision
> Could make doubtful selectors think now ... er ...

> The skill of the great Bearded Wonder
> Embraces all facts without blunder.
>   Who, how, when and what
>   By which ball and what shot
> And, when dead, how far buried under.

And Mrs Patricia Dawes provided us with this touching postscript:

> Oh dear, the Tests have finished.
> Where has the summer gone?
> My life is now diminished
> Now TMS is done.
> Your comments and your chatter
> Delight us all at home;
> It almost doesn't matter
> If gloom and rain *does* come.
> Dear Freddie's pungent comments
> Get nods from all who hear;
> Whilst Brian's happy stories
> Give moments of great cheer.
> You're all such friendly people,
> So let me simply say
> Roll on, roll on next summer
> And bless you on your way.

Another word game is underway: B. J. and the Alderman at Old Trafford.

For most people – the crowd at the game, the audience at home – the excitement and action of a Test Match is going on out there in the middle. For two of our number, however, Brian Johnston and Don Mosey, the most tense contest is usually to be found at the back of the commentary box as they do battle with their word game. The rules are simple. A piece of paper and a pen or pencil each is all you need. In turn each contestant announces a letter of the alphabet (in the enforced silence of the box this is usually done by means of a pad of paper) and each letter is entered on both players' charts which are five squares by five. The object is to form words – ten points being gained for a five-letter word, five for four letters and one for three letters.

It is a source of great mystery to Don that Brian is so good at the game, despite playing it with characteristically merry abandon. The final score for 1984 was BJ 126, Don 63, 17 ties. During the Lord's Test though, Brian surprised even himself with an amazing score of 90 without recourse to his favourite words: TRUSS and TRESS.

This is the winning effort; and bear in mind that with the same letters Don only managed 66!

C	L	A	S	S
L	I	G	H	T
A	N	A	O	I
M	E	T	E	R
P	R	E	S	S

We should be interested in anyone who manages the perfect 100 in a true competition!

The Third Test at Headingley
Fred Trueman

Headingley, the home of Yorkshire cricket, was the venue for the Third Test between England and the all-conquering West Indies team on July 12th through to July 17th. In our hearts and our prayers we hoped for an England victory but deep down inside we all knew that the mighty West Indies cricket machine, if the weather did not interrupt, would brush England aside in less than the allotted five days. This was a critical match for both England and the series – the tourists had already won the first two Tests quite handsomely, and if they were to win this one they would retain the Wisden Trophy and the series would be lost. The only interest thus remaining would be in whether the West Indies could go on and complete a whitewash, which had happened only twice before in the history of Test cricket, Australia versus England and England versus India. I arrived at the ground with all those statistics going round in my head, thinking to myself 'What can England do to rekindle their shattered confidence and sagging morale, knowing that the Headingley wicket is so helpful to seam and swing bowlers these days?'

I did not have to wait long to make up my mind. Just one look at the wicket was enough to tell me that England were going to be up against superior forces from the start. In 37 years of association with Headingley, I have never seen anything like what I saw on that morning of July 12th. Due to no rain for weeks the outfield was of a light brown colour more befitting a stage set for a scene from *The Desert Song* than a cricket match. The actual square itself was like a giant emerald standing out in a drought-ridden land that must have had every seam and swing bowler from Birmingham to Barbados straining at the leash to get on to it. I could not believe it – even I, at my old age, was tempted to go and see the selectors in the hope that they might just slip me into the side for one last fling. The looking-glass of memory might be dimming but for a moment it was a delightful thought.

That daydream was shattered as quickly as it had appeared by the West Indies crowd who had gathered under the score-board at the Kirkstall end in brilliant sunshine with their drums, bugles and anything else they had been able to find to make an annoying all-day noise so discomforting to other spectators. After the now customary ritual of exercises by the England side, led by Bernie Thomas, the physiotherapist, we were getting close to the time for the captains to come out to toss the coin, enabling us to see what decisions or strategy had been made. It was an absolute certainty that those of the selectors and senior players would differ from the views of Trevor Bailey, Brian Johnston and myself, with Tony Cozier quietly chuckling to himself in the background. The answer to all our thoughts rapped out over the air was given when D. Gower, the England captain, won the toss and decided to bat first. It is a well-worn cliché that nine times out of ten when you win the toss you bat, and the tenth time you think about it and still take first use of the pitch. I felt sorry for the England batsmen having to face the most feared pace attack in the world on a pitch that was bound to be suited to their opponents. It was one of those pitches on which, no matter how well you batted (you could say to yourself 'I'm in for the day'), the odd delivery was bound to do something, either in the air or off the wicket, and get you out.

Opening bats Fowler and Broad, the latter in only his second Test, walked with an air of confidence to the wicket. If they had any nerves, and they must have had, they got full marks for the way they concealed them. The game started and the first ball was greeted with the traditional noise from the West Indian supporters. It starts like the utterings of a playful pup and finishes with a thunderous roar that would send the legendary Hound of the Baskervilles to the safety of its den. England were soon in the trouble forecast on this pitch. Fowler, who plays and misses the ball more often than any left-hander I can remember, was first to go after making 10. Paul Terry, making his debut for England, came in at number three. Why a young, inexperienced player was put in this situation I shall never know. Surely it would not have been too much to ask for a senior player like Gower himself or even Lamb to shoulder that responsibility? One thing I do know, and that is Headingley is not the place these days for a batsman to be playing in his first Test. I also suspect that Terry was only picked because earlier in the season he had made a century for his county, Hampshire, against Clarke of Surrey, a West Indian bowler at great pace on the slow batting wicket at The Oval. Terry's was the second wicket to fall after he had scored 8, and I must say the young man looked not only disappointed but sadly out of his class. I sometimes wonder what the selectors are looking for when they know full well the importance of batting at number three in a Test Match.

The England captain, David Gower, who had not been having a good season, came to the wicket. We were all hoping he could produce one of those innings of which we know he is capable. But it was not to be. After making only two, he padded up to a good length delivery, totally misreading the line. He did not get outside the off-stump and was out lbw, and England were in real trouble. At lunch on the first day they had reached 68 for 3 off 28 overs. One bit of sad news we learned during the lunch interval was that Marshall, the world's fastest bowler, who had left the field during the morning after fielding a harmless-looking ball at gully, had actually sustained a double fracture of the left thumb and was unlikely to return to the match. Sad news indeed, but it was now up to England to take full advantage of this mishap. It did not seem to worry the West Indies – they still had three fast bowlers in Garner, Holding and Baptiste to build on their great start.

England's tale of woe continued after lunch. Opening batsman Broad, who had batted bravely for 32, was out and England had lost their fourth wicket with only 87 runs on the score-board. Botham now entered the battleground. England's champion received tumultuous applause from the capacity crowd as he joined Lamb who was playing with great confidence at the other end.

The runs started to flow at a fast pace as Lamb and Botham took everything the West Indies let them have. Could this be the revival we were all looking for? Was the absence of Marshall from the attack starting to work in England's favour as West Indian captain Lloyd started to juggle his bowlers around in desperate search of a wicket? The partnership had produced 85 runs in 76 minutes. That had the crowd excited and had quietened the drums and the bugles at the Kirkstall end.

But Lady Luck deserted England in her hour of need. Botham, who had made 45, tried to get inside a lifting ball from Baptiste down the leg-side. Unluckily for him it flicked his glove, and wicket-keeper Dujon brought off a magnificent one-handed catch to end a wonderful partnership. England were now 172 for 5. Downton, England's wicket-keeper, who was having a good series, joined Lamb, who was now proving he was our best batsman. At tea England were 180 for 5. Lamb was on 60 not out. 'With a bit of care' I was thinking, 'if England can make 300 on this pitch in their first innings they might just have an outside chance of bringing about a shock result.' The West Indies had only one success between tea and close of play, Downton being out for 17. Lamb had completed a fine century and stumps were drawn with England at the end of the first day's play in the healthy position of 237 for 6.

The second day brought a shock for England in the first over. Lamb, who had played so brilliantly, was out clean bowled by Harper, playing a terrible shot giving himself room to cut against the spin. A sad end to a great innings. The tail-enders were soon snapped up, only Pringle, who made 19, showing any resistance, and England were all out for 270. They should have made a lot more. Holding, with 4 for 70 off 29.2 overs, had been the West Indies' most successful bowler. He had been well supported by Harper (3 for 47 off 19 overs) and Garner (2 for 73 off 30), making up for the loss of Marshall through his unfortunate injury.

The West Indies' first innings got off to a bad start for them, both openers going with only 43 runs on the board. The mighty Richards went soon after lunch for only 15 with a total on 78; Allott, who had been recalled to the Test team, the man causing concern. He was bowling line and length and letting the ball do the work, as you should do. A stand of 70 by captain Lloyd and Gomes put the West Indies back into the game before Cook had Lloyd caught bat and pad with a total on 148. They had lost their fourth wicket. Allott came back into the attack and quickly put England back into the driving seat, grabbing 3 wickets to destroy the West Indies' middle batting order.

At close of play on the second day the West Indies had clawed their way back into the game due to a fine 79 not out by Gomes ably assisted by Holding on 28 not out. We all looked forward eagerly to the third day, right behind England. Could they get a first innings lead? News had arrived that Marshall would take no further part in the match, so in effect the West Indies had 8 wickets down with only Garner to come in and England still

The one-armed bandit of Headingley. Malcolm Marshall – left hand in plaster – still carves Allott for 4.

had a lead of 31 precious runs. Nobody expected on the Headingley wicket what was to happen. It was unbelievable. Holding set about Willis and gave him one of the biggest hidings he has ever had in his life, hooking and pulling him for three sixes in one over. Willis had to be taken off and Allott brought on in his place. It turned out to be a good move. The Lancashire bowler had Holding out, caught for 59. He had hammered five sixes and three fours off 55 balls in a stand worth 82 runs in 72 minutes with partner Gomes, who was on 98 not out. Garner was run out for 0 trying to give the bowling to Gomes. Much to our surprise, some West Indian players appeared on the balcony and told Gomes to stay at the wicket, Marshall was coming in to bat. What a marvellous gesture! Marshall said that Gomes deserved his 100, and on that wicket I agreed with him. Gomes completed his century, and Marshall sneaked a 4 one-handed through the slips before he was out, off Allott with a total on 302.

Allott had the best figures of his Test career with 6 for 62 off 26.5 overs. Gomes, 104 not out, had steered West Indies to a first innings lead of 32 which should never have been seen. The most amazing thing to me in the match so far was that on a seam bowler's pitch Botham, England's champion all-rounder, had only bowled at 7 overs for 45 runs. No wonder they say cricket is a funny game. The other thing that stood out was the pathetic sight of Willis, still trying his heart out, but being thrashed by batsmen he would have beaten two seasons earlier. He finished with 2 wickets for 123 runs off 18 overs.

England's second innings had a disastrous start. Marshall, who had decided he was fit enough to bowl, had Broad caught for 2, Garner had new boy Terry out for 1 and England were 13 for 2. Fowler and Gower managed to salvage some of England's pride, and at tea had taken the score to 85 for 2. Both of them had been on 37 not out, in fact they added 91 runs in 126 minutes to put England back into the game with just a slim chance. Gower was the first to go in the partnership after tea when he had made 43 and the total was 104 for 3. Fowler completed his half-century before he was caught and bowled by Marshall with his injured thumb in plaster. It was at this point that tragedy struck. Lamb, the first innings century-maker, was out to Marshall lbw for 3 and England had lost half their side for 107 and were only 75 runs ahead. The mighty Botham was on his way to the wicket and memories of his blistering century on the same ground against Australia two years earlier came flooding back. Could he do it again? It was a short-lived memory – he was out for 14, caught behind the wicket to a lifting ball. He was unlucky to get a touch which for me was the best delivery of the match. At the close of play England were 136 for 6, a lead of 104.

On the fourth day, England's tail held out for another half-hour before they were all back in the pavilion for 159, leaving the West Indies to score 128 to win the match and the Wisden Trophy. Marshall, who was to have taken no further part in the match according to a press release, had the amazing figures of 7 for 57 off 26 overs, and was immediately labelled 'the one-armed bandit'. It had been a most astonishing performance. Greenidge (49) and Haynes (43) had taken the total to 74 for no wickets at lunch and the writing was on the wall for England. Left-hand spinner Cook grabbed both openers but the Test was hopeless. Richards (22 not out) and Garner (2 not out) saw the West Indies through to 131 for 2 and the tourists had won by 8 wickets.

Little did we know then that it was to be the end of Willis's Test career. We appreciate what he has done for his country, but it comes to us all sooner or later. We can all beat records but we cannot beat age. It was the great Yorkshire and England all-rounder George Herbert Hirst who once said 'bowlers win matches' and once again these words have been proved correct by the West Indies' fast-bowling battery. The only interest left in the series was could the West Indies complete a whitewash or could England save her pride by preventing it?

ENGLAND 1ST INNINGS v. WEST INDIES (3RD TEST) at HEADINGLEY, LEEDS on 12,13,14,16 JULY, 1984.

IN	OUT	MINS	No.	BATSMAN	HOW OUT	BOWLER	RUNS	WKT	TOTAL	6s	4s	BALLS	NOTES ON DISMISSAL TOSS: ENGLAND
11·00	11·36	36	1	G. FOWLER	LBW	GARNER	10	1	13	·	2	25	Mis)ndged line - padded up to ball that 'straightened'
11·00	2·08	168	2	B.C. BROAD	C⁺ LLOYD	HARPER	32	4	87	·	4	117	Edged backfoot square drive to 1ST slip
11·38	12·12	34	3	V.P. TERRY	C⁺ HARPER	HOLDING	8	2	43	·	1	25	Edged outswinger low to 3RD slip's right.
12·14	12·30	16	4	D.I. GOWER *	LBW	GARNER	2	3	53	·		13	Played no stroke to ball that came back and flicked pad.
12·32	11·05	228	5	A.J. LAMB	BOWLED	HARPER	100	7	237	·	15	186	Off-break kept low - missed back foot cover-drive.
2·10	3·26	76	6	I.T. BOTHAM	C⁺ DUJON	BAPTISTE	45	5	172	1	7	61	Legside catch - followed short ball - ball hit gloves.
3·28	5·10	83	7	P.R. DOWNTON †	C⁺ LLOYD	HARPER	17	6	236	·	2	54	Edged off-drive to 1ST slip.
5·12	12·19	82	8	D.R. PRINGLE	C⁺ HAYNES	HOLDING	19	10	270	·	3	74	HOLDING'S 200TH TEST WICKET. Mishooked skier to mid-wicket.
11·06	11·24	18	9	P.J.W. ALLOTT	BOWLED	HOLDING	3	8	244	·	·	16	Off stump out - beaten by pace.
11·26	11·50	24	10	N.G.B. COOK	BOWLED	HOLDING	1	9	254	·	·	22	Beaten by outswinger that clipped off stump.
11·51	(12·19)	28	11	R.G.D. WILLIS	NOT OUT		4			·	·	13	54TH 'not out' - world Test record extended.

✳ CAPTAIN † WICKET-KEEPER   **EXTRAS** b 4 lb 7 w – nb 18   **29**   1⁶ 34⁴ 606 balls (including 22 no balls)

TOTAL (97·2 OVERS; 394 MINUTES) **270** all out at 12·19 pm second day.

14 OVERS 5 BALLS/HOUR
2·77 RUNS/OVER
45 RUNS/100 BALLS

BOWLER	O	M	R	W	nb		HRS	OVERS	RUNS
GARNER	30	11	73	2	14	1	14	28
MARSHALL	6	4	6	0	1	2	14	40
HOLDING	29·2	8	70	4	4	3	15	40
BAPTISTE	13	1	45	1	4	4	16	72
HARPER	19	6	47	3	·	5	14	44
			29			6	15	29
	97·2	30	270	10				

2ND NEW BALL taken at 11·43 am 2nd day
- ENGLAND 253-8 off 88 overs.

RUNS	MINS	OVERS	LAST 50 (in mins)
50	85	20	85
100	172	41·3	87
150	212	51·5	40
200	269	65·5	57
250	349	85·4	80

LUNCH: 68-3 (28 OVERS / 120 MIN.) BROAD 26* (120') LAMB 7* (28')
TEA: 180-5 (59 OVERS / 240 MIN.) LAMB 60* (148') DOWNTON 2* (12')
STUMPS: 237-6 (77 OVERS / 315 MIN.) (1ST DAY) 8·15P.m at 5·15pm (45 kap) LAMB 100* (223') PRINGLE 1* (3')

WKT	PARTNERSHIP		RUNS	MINS
1ST	Fowler	Broad	13	36
2ND	Broad	Terry	30	34
3RD	Broad	Gower	10	16
4TH	Broad	Lamb	34	56
5TH	Lamb	Botham	85	76
6TH	Lamb	Downton	64	83
7TH	Lamb	Pringle	1	8
8TH	Pringle	Allott	7	18
9TH	Pringle	Cook	10	24
10TH	Pringle	Willis	16	28

Compiled by BILL FRINDALL

WEST INDIES 1ST INNINGS   IN REPLY TO ENGLAND'S 270 ALL OUT

IN	OUT	MINS	No.	BATSMAN	HOW OUT	BOWLER	RUNS	WKT	TOTAL	6s	4s	BALLS	NOTES ON DISMISSAL
12·31	12·56	25	1	C.G. GREENIDGE	C⁺ BOTHAM	WILLIS	10	1	16	·	2	23	Edged low to second slip.
12·31	2·06	55	2	D.L. HAYNES	BOWLED	ALLOTT	18	2	43	·	2	35	Bowled through gate attempting an on drive.
12·58	(12·58)	314	3	H.A. GOMES	NOT OUT		104			·	14	197	(7TH in TESTS)
2·08	2·27	19	4	I.V.A. RICHARDS	C⁺ PRINGLE	ALLOTT	15	3	78	·	2	12	Mistimed on-drive - head-high catch to mid-on.
2·29	4·18	88	5	C.H. LLOYD *	C⁺ GOWER	COOK	48	4	148	·	7	75	Silly point catch - ball hit glove via pad.
4·20	5·20	60	6	P.J. DUJON †	LBW	ALLOTT	26	5	201	·	4	52	Hit across line (on drive) of full length ball.
5·22	5·29	7	7	E.A.E. BAPTISTE	C⁺ BROAD	ALLOTT	0	6	206	·	·	4	Drove wide half-volley to wide mid-off (2-handed catch to left)
5·31	5·32	1	8	R.A. HARPER	C⁺ DOWNTON	ALLOTT	0	7	206	·	·	2	Played inside straight ball - faint edge.
5·34	11·59	72	9	M.A. HOLDING	C⁺ ALLOTT	WILLIS	59	8	288	5	3	55	Hooked bouncer to long-leg. Well-judged catch.
12·01	12·08	7	10	J. GARNER	RUN OUT (TERRY/WILLIS)		0	9	290	·	·	1	Hesitated over second run to long-on (Gomes stroke).
12·10	12·58	16	11	M.D. MARSHALL	C⁺ BOTHAM	ALLOTT	4	10	302	·	·	8	Batted one-handed (right). Edged to 2nd slip.

✳ CAPTAIN † WICKET-KEEPER   **EXTRAS** b – lb 3 w – nb 15   **18**   5⁶ 35⁴ 464 balls (including 21 balls)

TOTAL (73·5 OVERS, 341 MINUTES) **302** all out at 12·58 pm on third day (LUNCH TAKEN).

13 OVERS 0 BALLS/HOUR
4·09 RUNS/OVER
65 RUNS/100 BALLS

BOWLER	O	M	R	W	nb		HRS	OVERS	RUNS
WILLIS	18	1	123	2	1	1	13	47
ALLOTT	26·5	7	61	6	·	2	12	67
BOTHAM	7	0	45	0	·	3	15	43
PRINGLE	13	3	26	0	10	4	14	49
COOK	9	1	29	1	·	5	12	56
			18					
	73·5	12	302	10				

RUNS	MINS	OVERS	LAST 50 (in mins)
50	64	13·3	64
100	107	22·3	43
150	175	39·1	68
200	227	51·5	52
250	283	63·1	56
300	333	72·0	50

LUNCH: 19-1 (7 OVERS / 31 MIN.) HAYNES 6* (31') GOMES 3* (4')
TEA: 138-3 (33 OVERS / 150 MIN.) GOMES 42* (142') LLOYD 46* (72')
STUMPS: 239-7 (60 OVERS / 269 MIN.) (2ND DAY) GOMES 79* (242') HOLDING 28* (27')

WKT	PARTNERSHIP		RUNS	MINS
1ST	Greenidge	Haynes	16	25
2ND	Haynes	Gomes	27	27
3RD	Gomes	Richards	35	19
4TH	Gomes	Lloyd	70	88
5TH	Gomes	DuJon	53	60
6TH	Gomes	Baptiste	5	7
7TH	Gomes	Harper	0	1
8TH	Gomes	Holding	82	72
9TH	Gomes	Garner	2	7
10TH	Gomes	Marshall	12	16

302

Compiled by BILL FRINDALL

ENGLAND 2ND INNINGS   32 RUNS BEHIND ON FIRST INNINGS

IN	OUT	MINS	No.	BATSMAN	HOW OUT	BOWLER	RUNS	WKT	TOTAL	6s	4s	BALLS	NOTES ON DISMISSAL
1·40	4·52	160	1	G. FOWLER	c't AND BOWLED	MARSHALL	50	4	106	·	9	128	Held hard waist-high catch two-handed.
1·40	1·51	11	2	B.C. BROAD	c't BAPTISTE	MARSHALL	2	1	10	·	·	9	Fended sharply lifting ball to backward square leg.
1·54	2·03	9	3	V.P. TERRY	LBW	GARNER	1	2	13	·	·	8	Missed push across line of straight full-length ball.
2·05	4·43	126	4	D.I. GOWER *	c't DUJON	HARPER	43	3	104	·	8	100	Pushed forward - edged off-break to 'keeper.
4·45	4·58	13	5	A.J. LAMB	LBW	MARSHALL	3	5	107	·	·	6	Hit on back leg. Late on break-back - through 'gate'.
4·54	5·57	63	6	I.T. BOTHAM	c't DUJON	GARNER	14	6	135	·	2	50	Offside edge - 'walked'.
5·00	11·30	92	7	P.R. DOWNTON †	c't DUJON	MARSHALL	27	10	159	·	4	67	Edged off-drive high to 'keeper.
5·59	11·09	12	8	N.G.B. COOK	c't LLOYD	MARSHALL	0	7	138	·	·	13	Tried to withdraw bat from outswinger - 1st slip - diving to right.
11·10	11·12	2	9	D.R. PRINGLE	LBW	MARSHALL	2	8	140	·	·	3	Beaten by break-back. Shuffled across stumps.
11·13	11·19	6	10	P.J.W. ALLOTT	LBW	MARSHALL	4	9	146	·	1	4	Played back to full-length low break-back.
11·21	(11·30)	9	11	R.G.D. WILLIS	NOT OUT		5			·	1	4	55th 'not out' - extended his world Test record.
* CAPTAIN † WICKET-KEEPER				EXTRAS	b - lb 6	w - nb 2	8			0s 25 4s		392 balls (including 2 no balls)	

TOTAL (65 OVERS, 260 MINUTES)   159 All out at 11·30 am on 4th day.

15 OVERS 0 BALLS/HOUR
2·45 RUNS/OVER
41 RUNS/100 BALLS

BOWLER	O	M	R	W	nb		HRS	OVERS	RUNS
MARSHALL	26	9	53	7	1	1	1	14	34
GARNER	16	7	37	2	·	2	2	16	57
HOLDING	7	1	31	0	1	3	3	16	18
HARPER	16	8	30	1	·	4	4	14	28
			8						
	65	25	159	10					

RUNS	MINS	OVERS	LAST 50 (in mins)
50	81	19·0	81
100	135	34·4	54
150	252	63·0	117

TEA: 85-2 [27 OVERS / 109 MIN] FOWLER 37* (109') GOWER 37* (84')

STUMPS: 135-6 [58 OVERS / 230 MIN] DOWNTON 14* (62') COOK 0* (3')
3RD DAY   103 AHEAD

4TH DAY: ENGLAND LOST LAST FOUR WICKETS for 24 runs in 30 minutes off 7 overs - Marshall's best analysis in Tests (today 4-0-15-4) - with his doubly-fractured left thumb encased in plaster.

WKT	PARTNERSHIP		RUNS	MINS
1st	Fowler	Broad	10	11
2nd	Fowler	Terry	3	9
3rd	Fowler	Gower	91	126
4th	Fowler	Lamb	2	7
5th	Lamb	Botham	1	4
6th	Botham	Downton	28	57
7th	Downton	Cook	3	12
8th	Downton	Pringle	2	2
9th	Downton	Allott	6	6
10th	Downton	Willis	13	9
			159	

Compiled by BILL FRINDALL

WEST INDIES 2ND INNINGS   REQUIRING 128 TO WIN IN A MINIMUM OF 680 MINUTES.

IN	OUT	MINS	No.	BATSMAN	HOW OUT	BOWLER	RUNS	WKT	TOTAL	6s	4s	BALLS	NOTES ON DISMISSAL
11·41	2·33	131	1	C.G. GREENIDGE	c't TERRY	COOK	49	2	108	·	7	96	Edged via pad to forward short-leg - simple catch.
11·41	2·25	123	2	D.L. HAYNES	c't FOWLER	COOK	43	1	106	·	3	85	Edged on drive to extra-cover.
2·27	(2·48)	21	3	H.A. GOMES	NOT OUT		2			·	·	11	
2·35	(2·48)	13	4	I.V.A. RICHARDS	NOT OUT		22			·	4	18	Made winning hit.
			5	C.H. LLOYD *									
			6	P.J. DUJON †									
			7	E.A.E. BAPTISTE									
			8	R.A. HARPER	Did not bat								
			9	M.A. HOLDING									
			10	J. GARNER									
			11	M.D. MARSHALL									
* CAPTAIN † WICKET-KEEPER				EXTRAS	b - lb 2	w - nb 13	15			0s 14 4s		210 balls (including 15 no balls)	

TOTAL (32·3 OVERS, 146 MINUTES)   131-2

13 OVERS 2 BALLS/HOUR
4·03 RUNS/OVER
62 RUNS/100 BALLS

BOWLER	O	M	R	W	nb		HRS	OVERS	RUNS
WILLIS	8	1	40	0	10	1	1	12	50
ALLOTT	7	2	24	0	·	2	2	15	52
COOK	9	2	27	2					
PRINGLE	8·3	2	25	0	5				
			15						
	32·3	7	131	2					

RUNS	MINS	OVERS	LAST 50 (in mins)
50	59	11·5	59
100	119	26·4	60

LUNCH: 74-0 [15 OVERS / 79 MINUTES] GREENIDGE 35* HAYNES 29*

WEST INDIES WON BY 8 WICKETS AT 2·48 pm on the fourth day and so retaining the SIR FRANK WORRELL TROPHY

MAN OF THE MATCH : H.A. GOMES
Adjudicator: A.R. LEWIS

TOTAL TIME LOST : 1 HOUR 42 MINUTES

WKT	PARTNERSHIP		RUNS	MINS
1st	Greenidge	Haynes	106	123
2nd	Greenidge	Gomes	2	6
3rd	Gomes	Richards	23*	13
			131	

Compiled by BILL FRINDALL

PETER BAXTER

The man who fulfilled his boyhood dream: BBC Cricket Correspondent, Christopher Martin-Jenkins.

SO YOU WANT TO BE A COMMENTATOR?
Christopher Martin-Jenkins

The letters come in all sorts of different styles, some written by hand, some carefully typed, from a wide variety of age-groups and from all parts of Britain. Though some get to the point at once and others take a circuitous route, the gist of what they want to ask is much the same: how do I become a cricket journalist, and, in some cases, also a cricket commentator?

I try to answer them all and occasionally I suggest that someone should come to see me. I do not forget that when I had just left school and was Cambridge bound, Brian Johnston, partly perhaps because he liked my letter and knew I had done reasonably well in school cricket, but partly also because I was the son of a friend of a friend, kindly asked me to Broadcasting House where, in an office shared with Raymond Baxter and decorated mainly with naughty holiday postcards, he gave me some words of cheery encouragement before taking me over the road to the BBC Club for a salad and a glass of white wine. He left me under no illusion that it would be easy to break into cricket broadcasting but he stressed the need to keep playing and to practise commentating whenever I could.

It was essential advice, although really I did not need it because from the age of about eight my great passion in life had been cricket and, whenever I was playing in anything other than serious matches, I used to give a running commentary under my breath. Brian advised me to start going to first-class matches with a tape recorder and this I did, although I used to feel a bit of a twerp if I was sitting near anyone in the crowd and talking to myself, so my efforts were rather similar to that chap – is it Arthur Lowe or Ted Lowe? – who does the snooker commentaries on television: all very hushed and intimate. There was a trace, too, of Henry Longhurst's reverential tones around the golfing greens, although not, alas, his ginny voice, easy command of vocabulary or rich fund of anecdotes.

My own break came when E. W. Swanton, then a revered name, later a greatly respected and warmly sympathetic mentor, took a gamble with my enthusiasm, ignored my inexperience and made me Assistant Editor of *The Cricketer*. There is probably some truth in the soccer manager's cliché that 'you make your own luck in this game' but this, undoubtedly, was a large slice of fortune which I was determined to make the most of. *Everyone* needs luck.

John Arlott always says that he more or less fell into cricket commentating. No doubt he did, in which case full marks go to those who saw his genius for it but, having been given the opportunity, he obviously needed no second invitation. Nor, I imagine, did Neville Cardus when he started writing about cricket for the Manchester *Guardian*. The average mortal, unlike these exceptional talents, has to want to be a cricket commentator very much indeed if he is ever going to become one. If an apple tree only produces a few ripe or rosy fruits, only a fit, determined and hungry person is going to climb the tree and claim one for himself!

It hardly needs saying that anyone aspiring to commentate on cricket needs a true devotion to the game. The fraudulent 'cricket lover' will always give him-(or her-) self away. To be able to interpret a match fairly, a commentator needs to have played the game a good deal – how else can he identify with those taking part? – and obviously the higher the level played, the better, so the would-be commentator should play as much cricket as he can. Any cricket is better than none and, although age eventually wins, that remains true for those actually doing the job. For instance, at the end of the 1983 season I found myself invited to

captain West Surrey in the festival for club cricketers held each September at the headquarters of the county's cricket, an excellent idea. Although only a truncated limited-overs match, it was a valuable reminder to me of all sorts of things one ought to be bearing in mind when describing first-class cricket; for example, just how marvellous it can be to bat on a good, professionally prepared pitch; how difficult it can be to sight the ball on gloomy days in large grounds with seating all round the perimeter; how out-fields which look dry from a distance can in fact be sopping wet; and how captains rely on their bowlers. The opposition needed 30 to win off the last two 8-ball overs, 18 to win off the last one, and 1 off the very last ball. I am afraid they got them! During those 2 overs I twice foresaw the possibility of a 4 being scored in two particular gaps in the out-field but twice plugged the gaps only *after* 4s had been scored there. But if that was my fault, deserving of criticism had there been someone watching from the commentary box, the dropped catch in the out-field by the long-on who saw the ball too late and let it carry over his head with 2 balls of the match left, was crucial. And whose fault was that? It was a salutary reminder to be as sympathetic as possible when comfortably placed behind a microphone.

So, even to become a commentator – let alone a good one – you need luck, determination, a genuine love of cricket, and the will and ability to play the game as often as you can. You must also know and remember the history of cricket, if you are to place any performance you are describing into its proper context, as well as having a thorough knowledge of the laws of the game and of any special regulations applying to whatever match is being played. An awareness of the topical significance of the game in question and as close a knowledge as possible of the players, their characters, records, and methods are also important. This is another way of saying, really, that you have got to know what you are talking about. Again, the listener will soon spot someone who doesn't.

To know cricket inside out is essential, but in itself still not enough. Much more goes on at a cricket match than just the game itself, especially in a Test Match, and the greater the education, both worldly and academic, of the commentator, the more interesting and rounded his description of events is likely to be. Good commentary is more subjective than objective: simply running an eye round a cricket ground and describing the landmarks in order to 'fill in' between the delivery of one ball and the next is often, for example, less effective than some relevant diversion, the type in which Brian Johnston specialises. Commentating is not just the ability to use words effectively to describe a scene; it is also a personal interpretation, a process of thinking out loud: the more interesting the thought, the more interested the listener is going to be. Above all, the process should be natural. If it suddenly strikes you that, say, St Paul's Cathedral is glinting in the sunshine in the distance, by all means say so, but *because* it has just struck you that this is so, not because a little voice inside says: right, now I will go round the ground and tell you everything I can see.

The art of 'natural' cricket commentary has been greatly aided in recent years by the more even flow between commentator and 'expert' summariser who was once religiously called in at the end of each over, often to state the obvious about the 6 balls just past. Now he may take up, at any convenient moment, a theme or a technical point; he may be reminded of an anecdote, or digress on any relevant topic.

Some of these things will come only with experience, but the would-be commentator needs first to master the nuts and bolts of the job. It is, after all, the first duty of any ball-by-ball commentator to give the score, say who is batting against whom, to describe every ball and to up-date the score at least every time a run is scored and at the end of each over. Moreover, although the casual listener might not care too much whether Emburey is bowling off-spin with a five-four field or leg-spin with five slips and a gully, the knowledgeable listener does want to *know* what the bowler is trying to bowl, the length and direction of the ball being described, whether the stroke was played off front foot or back, etc, etc. Like all things in cricket, as in life, it is a question of trying to get the right balance – in the case of commentary the balance between correct, accurate description and entertaining and informative background material. So the advice is not just to know cricket inside out, but also to know as much about as many other things in life as possible.

It would be easy to overlook the most important of all the necessities for would-be cricket commentators: a voice which is pleasing to listen to. Commentary stints are usually of 20 minutes' duration so the voice needs to attract and hold the attention – which does not necessarily mean it has to make you turn the volume down! A commentator needs to be easy to listen to over a long period and not therefore too monotonous, and he needs also to have some variety, some 'light and shade' in his voice. It is as important for the voice to be free of mannerisms that annoy as it is for the commentator to avoid clichés, constantly repeated phrases and whatever commentators' jargon happens to be in vogue at the time. Recent ones to steer clear of have been: 'For me, a great player ...'; 'In my book this has to go down as ...'; 'He's in all sorts of trouble', etc!

Three other things are worth bearing in mind as far as Test Match Special is concerned. A sense of humour is essential; it doesn't pay to be too self-important; and it helps if you are a connoisseur of cakes!

Sports journalism generally and cricket commentary in particular are professions to which many are called and few chosen. Those of us who got the lucky break are duly grateful. Although many are bound to be disappointed, if you love the game and are confident you could do the job, well, as the Australians say, 'Go for your life, mate'.

The Fourth Test at Old Trafford
Bill Frindall

A scene of utter chaos greeted our arrival at the door of our brand-new commentary box perched on the roof of the New Executive Suite at the Stretford end. Peter Baxter, surrounded by cases, papers and piles of assorted broadcasting equipment, was desperately trying to prepare for the start of our transmission less than an hour away. Three engineers were re-positioning cables, microphones and the television monitor, while a fourth was attempting to repair the support mechanism to the windows which had broken the first time they were opened. At the centre of all this confused activity was a carpenter feverishly completing the fittings to our new home. In less than an hour he installed a notice board and a clutch of coat hooks, and re-built the door-closing mechanism so that it did not slam every time it was used.

Superb organisation, aided by a series of minor miracles, enabled the programme to start smoothly with commentator, summariser, statistician and producer all comfortably positioned. Our previous box, sited to our left in a cramped and airless attic above the old score-board, had been demolished. The discomfort of working in it had marred my attitude to Old Trafford, although it had been the scene of my debut 19 years ago. During our last broadcast there, for a Prudential World Cup game, it had housed four commentators, two summarisers, a producer and his secretary, myself, and Mike Carey's labrador, Major, which, disguised as a low blond heap, slept peacefully through the day under our table with its head next to the feet of the summariser. Mushtaq Mohammad, having a native distaste for dogs, was reluctant to sit close to this one and kept getting 'off mike'. Goodness knows what listeners thought when Mushy responded to a question from Chris Martin-Jenkins about Javed Miandad's running between the wickets by squealing: 'He's licking my leg!'

Significant changes were not restricted to our commentary position. Bob Willis, whose 6 wickets in the first three Tests had cost 61.16 runs each, had been compelled to withdraw from the England team because of a recurrence of the virus infection that had caused his premature return from Pakistan in March. Twice this 35-year-old veteran of 90 Test matches had fought off crippling knee injuries to become the second highest wicket-taker in Test cricket. Sadly, his last first-class appearance coincided with England's humiliating defeat at Leeds where, three years earlier, he had bowled Mike Brearley's team to a sensational victory against Australia with an analysis of 8 for 43.

Norman Cowans, omitted after being twelfth man for the previous two Tests (did he drop a drink?), was recalled in place of Willis, and Kent's highly promising all-rounder, Richard Ellison, was eventually given the duties of reserve fielder. The most exciting change in selectorial policy concerned the choice of off-spinner. After ignoring him for 86 Tests while

they employed Miller, Greig, Willey, Cope, Emburey, Hemmings and Marks, the selectors at long last recalled Pat Pocock. Only Les Jackson (96 Tests) had had to endure a longer interval between appearances.

'Percy' Pocock was on stage immediately as the West Indies won the toss and took first innings for the first time in nine Tests. They were without Malcolm Marshall, their one-armed bandit from Headingley, although his plaster cast had been removed in the hope that his thumb had mended sufficiently to include him. His place was taken by Winston Davis, excluded from the original touring party and now on loan from Glamorgan.

A hazy day of light cloud gave way to blazing sun as Ian Botham bowled the first over. Although he had failed to take a wicket in the previous Test it was thought that Botham's ability to swing the ball late would be aided by the hot, steamy atmosphere. He struck both batsmen's pads twice in his first 5 balls and Fred Trueman was swift to ask why Ellison, with his late out-swing, had been left in the dressing-room. He also wondered why Allott, following his 6 wickets at Headingley, had not been given the new ball. We all wondered what FS would have said if he had been demoted to first change but wisely we kept quiet.

It was soon obvious that this was a very good toss to win. Just how vital we were not to know until the second innings. Cowans' first over showed us the pace of both the pitch and the out-field. The pitch was very, very slow and the parched out-field was lightning fast. Greenidge leaned effortlessly into a straightish off-drive and then had all the time in the world to cut a short ball wide of the cordon of slips. Poor Cowans: left out in the cold at his home ground, he found himself brought back on a pitch that offered him nothing.

Botham, whose letter to the TCCB announcing that he would not be available for England's winter tour had just been made public, showed in his second over why he would be sorely missed in India. Even when he does not look particularly dangerous he has the knack of taking wickets. As his final ball he offered Haynes a juicy long-hop which the batsman engagingly deposited down long-leg's throat.

England's rejoicing was short-lived. No sooner had FS revealed his amazement that Haynes should have fallen for such an old trick (I think his words were: 'I simply do not know what is going off out there!'), than Gomes acquired 3 boundaries from his first 5 balls. Cowans, still celebrating his beautifully-judged running catch, found the edge twice, only for the ball to fall short of the slips and race past the vacant third man position. Fred shifted his amazement to the field placing.

I shifted mine to the design of this new box. The windows were so high that we needed to sit on stools to have a clear view of the play. This meant that books kept in cases on the floor could not be reached from a sitting position. There were no shelves as in most of the other boxes, but fortunately I had brought a small side table. A new problem presented itself when Haynes was out and, in stopping the watch that timed his innings, I knocked the frame holding all three watches down a three-inch gap between the table and the wall. Luckily no damage was done but it did produce extra pressure at the busiest time for a scorer. Throughout that first day I had to be very careful not to lose items down the back of this ridiculously narrow working surface. Whoever designs commentary boxes can never have been near an outside broadcast. I managed to find our carpenter during the lunch interval and a full-size working surface awaited my arrival on the second morning.

England's brief moments of ascendancy during this difficult series had usually occurred some way into the contests. This time they came in the second hour with Paul Allott's eventual summons to the bowling crease. Spurred on by his home crowd he induced catches from Gomes and Richards in his third over. Two months earlier Richards had destroyed England's attack with an astonishing innings of 189 not out in the Texaco Trophy. Now he had been removed third ball. Lloyd followed a few minutes later. West Indies 70 for 4; Allott 4.1-2-10-3. His wickets had come in 13 balls for the cost of 5 runs. He must have lunched well.

Lunch is a vital interval for me. A break from the box is essential if concentration is to be maintained throughout the full six hours of play. A friend had prepared a tasty picnic at the far end of the roof and I was able to relax for half an hour in glorious sunshine. My work in the TMS box is very akin to my duties in the NATO war-room beneath a French forest in the early Sixties, the main difference being that then we worked only four-hour shifts!

After lunch Greenidge and Dujon settled down to repair the shattering start to their innings. They did so to such effect that they were not parted until six minutes before the close. Both reached their centuries before Botham, armed with the second new ball, surprised Dujon with a bouncer which he deflected gently to his wicket-keeping counterpart. It had been a good day for my colleagues. The pre-lunch dramas had given way to some excellent cricket afterwards. Greenidge's innings had been vastly different in character to his epic savagery of Lord's. He played straight and unleashed a series of superb drives when the right ball arrived. Dujon played with great fluency from the start. He has usually looked very confident and has a full armoury of handsome and stylish strokes. This time he got the selection process right. The commentator's bonus came in the form of 41 overs of spin from Nick Cook (20-5-39-0) and Pat Pocock (21-4-60-0). At long last England had restored a balanced attack. Although they met with no success, they caused many a problem on the slow pitch with its uneven bounce, and gave us that special entertainment that only the slow bowler's art can offer.

This match marked the centenary of Test cricket in Manchester. Old Trafford had received a face-lift during the winter. Apart from the New Executive Suite below us, which was formally opened before the third day's play by the Lord-Lieutenant of Greater Manchester, new shops and a cricket museum had been built beneath a stand at the Warwick Road end. The Lancashire committee's efforts had been rewarded with a large crowd, excellent cricket and a perfect summer's day – all in stark contrast to their very first day of Test cricket which had been totally washed out.

The second day was dominated by Gordon Greenidge. Displaying remarkable powers of concentration and abetted by the night-watchman, Winston Davis, he guided West Indies into an invincible position. Their partnership of 170 ensured a massive total and was a tribute to Greenidge's control of the situation. Davis, a tall man of near matchstick leanness, appropriately chose Lowry's Manchester as the stage for the highest innings of his first-class career. Despite the poor light that caused two pre-lunch interruptions totalling 45 minutes, both batsmen looked ominously comfortable from the start against Botham and Allott.

The breaks in play allowed a number of listeners' letters to be answered. One concerned a typical Johnstonian gaffe which had reduced us to hysteria at Leeds. Derek Pringle had been no-balled for the umpteenth time and BJ asked me how many times he had been called for over-stepping. When I told him he replied: 'Good Lord. And he had no balls at Lord's, didn't he?'

Now BJ was able to read a letter from a patient whose return to consciousness following a hernia operation had coincided with that remark. The resultant damage had required further surgery and an extra fortnight in hospital.

Two more breaks for rain and darkness took us into overtime and it was 6.56 pm when the West Indies innings ended neatly at 500. Pat Pocock celebrated his return by claiming 4 wickets. After being on 47 for eight years he had at last passed the 50-mark.

Saturday's start was delayed by rain until after an early lunch. Ironically, we had all assembled an hour before the scheduled start for a photo-call for this book. It was what E. W. Swanton would have described as a grizzly morning. Light rain and murky light. Sir Bernard Lovell, the Manchester University based radio-astronomer who had the vision and enterprise to build the 250-foot radio-telescope at Jodrell Bank, had installed experimental light-meters on the top of each sight-screen. Their output was displayed on two large dials mounted above the stand opposite the pavilion. The dials looked like the top half of a clockface, with '12' being the norm. The '9-12' arc indicated poor light and the '12-1' sector was playable-to-good. Strangely the umpires seem to ignore them.

After a few alarms – Broad was missed in the slips when 4 and Fowler was struck on the back of the helmet a couple of overs later – England survived the new ball spells of Garner and Davis. The latter produced some extremely sharp deliveries, including the one that severely tested Fowler's headgear. An on-field examination by Bernard Thomas confirmed that no damage had been done.

Because of the early lunch and delayed start, play was extended until 7.00 pm and tea postponed until 4.10 pm. The post-lunch session lasted two hours 37 minutes and proved a severe trial of concentration. Fortunately only 1 wicket fell, Fowler playing on via his left boot after 90 had been scored.

At tea we had a visit from Andrew Laidlaw, the Preston schoolboy who had spent two weeks in a coma during the summer of 1983 following a road accident. Brian and Fred had recorded messages for the nursing staff to play to him to help him regain consciousness as he was a regular TMS listener: not surprisingly, he had been shocked out of his coma.

No sooner had Andrew left us than Paul Terry's season was ended when he ducked into a short ball from Davis and was hit on the left forearm. Another visit from Bernard Thomas confirmed the damage as severe and it was found to be a fracture of the ulna. Broad, Gower, Botham and Downton fell before the close. With only 4 effective wickets left and arrears of 337 it looked like another innings defeat.

I drove down to Stratford on the rest day to play and commentate for the Lord's Taverners. The match, played on the attractive Town Cricket Ground beside the Avon, formed part of annual festival celebrations and was well attended. Basking in the hot sun the crowd were treated to a magnificent innings from Barry Richards. It was only his second knock since he had retired to take up golf 18 months previously. What a waste of a unique talent. Banned from the Test arena he had nothing to motivate him at first-class level.

His fellow South African, Allan Lamb, granted England status because of his Surrey-born parents, battled through the first session on Monday with night-watchman Allott supporting him for over an hour. After lunch Garner bowled Pocock and Cowans in his second over and Lamb, 98 not out, started to leave the field with the West Indies team. They were waved back by Gower and, three minutes after Cowans' demise, the pathetic figure of Terry, his broken arm in a sling beneath his sweater, stood at the bowler's end. Shortly before this a breakdown in transmission had occurred and we could only describe the dramatic events to a vacuum. Listeners were rescued by the expertise of studio announcer John Holmstrom, who gave a commentary from the television coverage. He described how Lamb took 2 runs to complete his 100 off the last ball of Holding's over, his third 100 in four innings in this series (a unique performance against the West Indies in England), before making to leave the field again. Once more they were turned back and Terry was left to face Garner one-handed. When asked why he didn't turn round and play him left-handed, Terry replied: 'I didn't want to break my other arm!'

He survived only one ball and, for the rest of the day, the TMS team debated the thinking behind Lamb taking a second run. Following on 220 behind, England were 120 for 5 (effectively 6) at the close. By lunch on Tuesday, Roger Harper had returned his best figures at Test level, West Indies had become the first touring side to win the first four matches of a rubber in England, and the TMS caravan was on its way home – cakes, sweets, side table and all.

Paul Terry – left arm broken – faces Joel Garner at Old Trafford.

WEST INDIES 1ST INNINGS v. ENGLAND (4TH TEST) at OLD TRAFFORD, MANCHESTER on 26,27,28,30,31 JULY, 1984.

IN	OUT	MINS	No.	BATSMAN	HOW OUT	BOWLER	RUNS	WKT	TOTAL	6s	4s	BALLS	NOTES ON DISMISSAL TOSS: WEST INDIES
11·00	6·30	588	1	C.G.GREENIDGE	c' DOWNTON	POCOCK	223	8	470	·	30	425	11th TESTS. (6th to score two 200s in a rubber.) HS in TESTS. Edged cut. Pocock's 5th wkt
11·00	11·12	12	2	D.L.HAYNES	c' COWANS	BOTHAM	2	1	11	·	·	9	Hooked long-hop high to long-leg. Running catch.
11·15	12·23	68	3	H.A.GOMES	c' BOTHAM	ALLOTT	30	2	60	·	5	59	Edged full-length offside ball low to 2nd slip.
12·25	12·28	3	4	I.V.A.RICHARDS	c' COOK	ALLOTT	1	3	62	·	·	3	Flicked full-length ball to mid-wicket.
12·30	12·45	15	5	C.H.LLOYD *	c' DOWNTON	ALLOTT	1	4	70	·	·	10	Edged push at off-stump ball via pad to 'keeper.
12·47	5·54	247	6	P.J.DUJON †	c' DOWNTON	BOTHAM	101	5	267	·	12	228	Attempted hook at bouncer skied gently off splice. (3rd in TESTS)
5·56	3·24	184	7	W.W.DAVIS	BOWLED	POCOCK	77	6	437	1	10	146	Nightwatchman. HS in F-C matches. Pushed at ball that hit off stump.
3·26	3·35	9	8	E.A.E.BAPTISTE	BOWLED	POCOCK	6	7	443	·	1	11	Made room to cut - then attempted pull. Ball kept low.
3·37	(6·56)	60	9	R.A.HARPER	NOT OUT		39			1	5	53	HS in TESTS
6·32	6·36	4	10	M.A.HOLDING	BOWLED	COOK	0	9	471	·	·	8	Bowled behind legs - missed sweep.
6·38	6·56	18	11	J.GARNER	c' TERRY	POCOCK	7	10	500	·	1	12	Edged off-break to forward short leg.

* CAPTAIN   † WICKET-KEEPER

EXTRAS: b 4 lb 6 w 2 nb 1 = 13   3 6s 63 4s 964 balls (including 1 no ball).

TOTAL (160·3 OVERS, 614 MINUTES) 500 all out at 6·56pm on 2nd day.

15 OVERS 4 BALLS/HOUR
3·12 RUNS/OVER
52 RUNS/100 BALLS

BOWLER	O	M	R	W	nb	w
BOTHAM	29	5	100	2	-/2	
COWANS	19	2	76	0	1/-	
ALLOTT	28	9	76	3	-	
COOK	39	6	114	1	-	
POCOCK	45·3	14	121	4	-	
			13			
	160·3	36	500	10		

2nd NEW BALL taken at 5·44 pm on 1st day.
WEST INDIES 264-4 after 89 overs.

HRS	OVERS	RUNS
1	13	45
2	12	31
3	16	60
4	17	61
5	17	47
6	18	29
7	13	47
8	19	60
9	17	57
10	15	35

RUNS	MINS	OVERS	LAST 50 (in mins)
50	75	16·2	75
100	146	32·2	71
150	189	43·5	43
200	248	60·3	59
250	316	80·0	68
300	409	103·4	93
350	450	115·0	41
400	499	131·0	49
450	568	149·0	69
500	613	160·2	45

LUNCH: 77-4 26 OVERS / 121 MIN. GREENIDGE 36 (121) DUJON 5 (14)
TEA: 198-4 59 OVERS / 242 MIN. GREENIDGE 90 (262) DUJON 76 (105)
STUMPS: 273-5 (1st DAY) 93 OVERS / 362 MIN. GREENIDGE 128 (402) DAVIS 2 (13)
LUNCH: 342-5 110 OVERS / 437 MIN. 45 MIN LOST (LIGHT) GREENIDGE 151 (437) DAVIS 47 (81)
TEA: 443-7 145 OVERS / 555 MIN. 2 MIN LOST (RAIN) GREENIDGE 214 (555) HARPER 0 (1)

WKT	PARTNERSHIP		RUNS	MINS
1st	Greenidge	Haynes	11	12
2nd	Greenidge	Gomes	49	68
3rd	Greenidge	Richards	2	3
4th	Greenidge	Lloyd	8	15
5th	Greenidge	Dujon	197	247
6th	Greenidge	Davis	170	184
7th	Greenidge	Baptiste	6	9
8th	Greenidge	Harper	27	34
9th	Harper	Holding	1	4
10th	Harper	Garner	29	18
			500	

Compiled by BILL FRINDALL

ENGLAND 1ST INNINGS   REQUIRING 301 RUNS TO AVOID FOLLOWING ON

IN	OUT	MINS	No.	BATSMAN	HOW OUT	BOWLER	RUNS	WKT	TOTAL	6s	4s	BALLS	NOTES ON DISMISSAL
1·33	3·53	140	1	G.FOWLER	BOWLED	BAPTISTE	38	1	90	·	5	112	Played on - edged drive via left boot into stumps.
1·33	5·11	195	2	B.C.BROAD	c' HARPER	DAVIS	42	2	112	·	3	146	Steered sharply lifting ball to 3rd slip (via Greenidge at 4th slip).
1·55 / 1·58	4·56 / 2·03	43	3	V.P.TERRY	BOWLED	GARNER	7	10 / 9	105 / 280	·	1	33	Left forearm (ulna) fractured by short ball from Davis. Retired 7*. Batted right-handed with no. 10 in sling under sweater.
4·58	5·17	19	4	D.I.GOWER *	c' DUJON	BAPTISTE	4	3	117	·	·	14	Flicked at offside ball. Firm-footed stroke. Low catch.
5·13	(2·03)	251	5	A.J.LAMB	NOT OUT		100			·	15	185	6th in TESTS - (3rd in 4 innings.
5·19	5·56	37	6	I.T.BOTHAM	c' GARNER	BAPTISTE	6	4	138	·	·	23	Sliced wide half-volley to gully - very high right-hand catch.
5·58	6·17	19	7	P.R.DOWNTON †	c' HARPER	GARNER	0	5	147	·	·	9	Edged onside push low to 3rd slip's left - ball 'left' him.
6·19	12·07	109	8	P.J.W.ALLOTT	c' GOMES	DAVIS	26	6	228	·	3	86	Miscued hook - gentle skier to backward square-leg.
12·09	12·44	35	9	N.G.B.COOK	BOWLED	HOLDING	13	7	257	·	3	29	Off stump - mis/nudged grope at ball angled in.
12·46	1·51	2	10	P.I.POCOCK	BOWLED	GARNER	0	8	278	·	·	14	Off stump.
1·53	1·55	2	11	N.G.COWANS	BOWLED	GARNER	0	9	278	·	·	4	Off stump.

* CAPTAIN   † WICKET-KEEPER

EXTRAS: b 5 lb 21 w - nb 18 = 44   0 6s 30 4s 655 balls (including 23 no balls).

TOTAL (105·2 OVERS, 448 MINUTES) 280 all out at 2·03 pm on 4th day.

14 OVERS 1 BALLS/HOUR
2·66 RUNS/OVER
43 RUNS/100 BALLS

BOWLER	O	M	R	W	nb
GARNER	22·2	7	51	4	4
DAVIS	20	2	71	2	14
HARPER	23	10	33	0	2
HOLDING	21	2	50	1	3
BAPTISTE	19	8	31	3	-
			44		
	105·2	29	280	10	

2nd NEW BALL taken at 11·56 am 4th day.
ENGLAND 212-5 after 85 overs.

HRS	OVERS	RUNS
1	13	40
2	18	41
3	15	24
4	10	33
5	15	24
6	14	50
7	14	53

RUNS	MINS	OVERS	LAST 50 (in mins)
50	82	20·1	82
100	163	42·1	81
150	271	63·1	108
200	350	82·2	79
250	402	95·0	52

TEA: 92-1 41 OVERS / 157 MIN BROAD 36 (157') TERRY 0 (15')
STUMPS: 163-5 (337 BEHIND) 73 OVERS / 305 MIN LAMB 27 (108') ALLOTT 10 (42')
LUNCH: 270-7 (230 BEHIND) 101 OVERS / 427 MIN LAMB 90 (230') POCOCK 0 (16')

WEST INDIES ENFORCED FOLLOW ON
- ENGLAND 220 BEHIND

WKT	PARTNERSHIP		RUNS	MINS
1st	Fowler	Broad	90	140
2nd	Broad	Terry / Gower	15 / 7	38 / 13
3rd	Gower	Lamb	5	4
4th	Lamb	Botham	21	37
5th	Lamb	Downton	9	19
6th	Lamb	Allott	81	109
7th	Lamb	Cook	29	35
8th	Lamb	Pocock	21	25
9th	Lamb	Cowans	0	2
10th	Lamb	Terry	2	5
			280	

Compiled by BILL FRINDALL

ENGLAND 2ND INNINGS   FOLLOWING ON 220 RUNS BEHIND

IN	OUT	MINS	No.	BATSMAN	HOW OUT	BOWLER	RUNS	WKT	TOTAL	6s	4s	BALLS	NOTES ON DISMISSAL
2.14	2.15	1	1	G. FOWLER	BOWLED	HOLDING	0	1	0	·	·	2	Played late half-cock push at breakback.
2.14	3.24	70	2	B.C. BROAD	LBW	HARPER	21	2	39	·	2	53	'Padded up' to 'arm' ball.
2.17	4.57	140	3	P.R. DOWNTON†	BOWLED	HARPER	24	3	77	·	3	115	Played on - edged drive via pad into stumps.
3.26	(12.11)	177	4	D.I. GOWER *	NOT OUT		57	·	·	·	8	153	His first 50 of the rubber.
4.59	5.27	28	5	A.J. LAMB	BOWLED	HARPER	9	4	99	·	1	27	Down wicket - missed on-drive - bowled via pad.
5.29	5.36	7	6	I.T. BOTHAM	C'T HAYNES	HARPER	1	5	101	·	·	8	Edged off break via pad to forward short leg - 'walked'.
5.38	11.36	30	7	P.J.W. ALLOTT	BOWLED	GARNER	14	6	125	·	3	28	Off stump removed - failed to play forward.
11.38	11.45	7	8	N.G.B. COOK	C' DUJON	GARNER	0	7	127	·	·	1	Followed away- seamer.
11.47	11.56	9	9	P.I. POCOCK	C' GARNER	HARPER	0	8	128	·	·	5	'PAIR' Drove to mid-off. HARPER'S BEST TEST ANALYSIS.
11.58	12.11	13	10	N.G. COWANS	BOWLED	HARPER	14	9	156	1	2	12	Missed vast swing to leg - ball rebounded off pads.
			11	V.P. TERRY	ABSENT HURT		·	·	·	·	·	·	Fractured left forearm.

*CAPTAIN   †WICKET-KEEPER   EXTRAS   b 9   lb 3   w 1   nb 3   16   1⁶ 19⁴ 404 balls (including 4 no balls)

TOTAL (66.4 OVERS, 249 MINUTES)   156 all out at 12.11 pm on the 5TH DAY.

16 OVERS 0 BALLS/HOUR
2.34   RUNS/OVER
39   RUNS/100 BALLS

BOWLER	O	M	R	W	w/nb	HRS	OVERS	RUNS
HOLDING	11	2	21	1	-/1	1	15	29
GARNER	12	4	25	2	1/-	2	17	47
HARPER	28.4	12	57	6	-/3	3	16	25
DAVIS	3	1	6	0	·	4	16	33
RICHARDS	1	0	2	0	·			
BAPTISTE	11	5	29	0	·			
			16					
	66.4	24	156	9				

	RUNS	MINS	OVERS	LAST 50 (in mins)
	50	86	22.4	86
	100	175	47.1	89
	150	248	66.2	73

TEA: 56-2 (164 BEHIND)   23 OVERS 87 MINUTES   DOWNTON 17*(84')   GOWER 15*(15')

STUMPS: 120-5 (4TH DAY) (100 BEHIND)   56 OVERS 208 MIN.   GOWER 43*(136')   ALLOTT 10*(24')

WEST INDIES WON BY AN INNINGS AND 64 RUNS - the first touring team to win the first 4 Tests of a rubber in England.

MAN OF THE MATCH: C.G. GREENIDGE
Adjudicator: E.R. DEXTER

TOTAL TIME LOST: 3 HOURS 10 MIN (NET)

WKT	PARTNERSHIP		RUNS	MINS
1st	Fowler	Broad	0	1
2nd	Broad	Downton	39	67
3rd	Downton	Gower	38	71
4th	Gower	Lamb	22	28
5th	Gower	Botham	2	7
6th	Gower	Allott	24	30
7th	Gower	Cook	2	7
8th	Gower	Pocock	1	9
9th	Gower	Cowans	28	13
			156	

compiled by BILL FRINDALL

VIEWS FROM THE BOUNDARY
Brian Johnston

Saturday lunch-times in the commentary box have been enlivened by a succession of personalities from the world of entertainment and sport. The only qualification needed is a love of cricket. Some of them have played, some still play, others just watch. In half an hour's conversation with them we have a lot of fun talking about themselves, and of course cricket.

Our first 'victim' of the 1984 season was Alan Curtis, actor, pantomime villain, Chairman of Old Time Music Hall at the Players' Theatre, and also the voice of the public address at five of the Test Match grounds. When he is unavailable his place is ably taken by comedian Johnny Dennis, also from the Players' Theatre. The only ground where neither of them perform is Edgbaston where for many years now Lyn Clugsden has been the 'voice of Edgbaston'. Alan has now done 74 Tests and funnily enough it all started way back in 1966 at Edgbaston where Alan was doing the public address for a match between the Lord's Taverners and an Old England XI. Unlike in Tests these days he was encouraged to be fairly light-hearted, and when he announced that 'the sun is shining on the rotunda', he added 'and I'm not referring to Stuart Surridge's waistline'. Leslie Deakins, then Secretary of Warwickshire, and Geoffrey Howard, the Surrey Secretary, both heard him that day. Up to then there had been no regular public address at Tests, just the occasional

---

For a commentator 'a sense of humour is essential,' says CMJ earlier in the book, 'and it doesn't pay to be too self-important'. To prove his point, here are a few of our *faux pas* which have caused much merriment both inside and outside the box:

'He's no mean slouch as a bowler.'   *Mike Denness*

'It's a catch he would have caught 99 times out of a thousand.'
                                                    Henry Blofeld

'There are good one-day players; there are good Test players – and vice versa ...'   *Trevor Bailey*

'... and Marshall throws his head to his hands!'
                                        Christopher Martin-Jenkins

'That was a tremendous six – the ball was still in the air as it went over the boundary.'   *Fred Trueman*

announcement by the Secretary. But both Leslie and Geoffrey thought what a good idea it would be to have someone permanently by a microphone to give details of the teams, announce in-going batsmen, give bowling figures etc. Geoffrey decided to try it out at The Oval that year in the Test versus the West Indies. Alan was working in a show so Clarrie Wright of Itma was the first person to do it.

Alan took over in 1967, and except for the odd stage or TV commitment has done it ever since. It's not an easy job to do. He must be informative to the crowd but *never* intrude on the play, and must resist the temptation to make jokes. He listens to Test Match Special and this did prompt him once to break his rule of non-interruption of play. It was during the Centenary Test at Lord's in 1980. He heard us all saying goodbye to John Arlott after John had just finished his last ever Test Match commentary. At the end of the next over Alan decided to announce that John had just ended his Test Match broadcasting career. The result was immediate. All the crowd stood up and applauded, and even the Australians in the field turned towards the pavilion and clapped. It was a moving moment for John and for all of us in the box, and Alan's initiative allowed the crowd to share it with us.

Although a fine actor Alan is I suppose best known for his superb portrayals of pantomime 'baddies' like the Sheriff of Nottingham, Abanazar and of course Captain Hook in Peter Pan. I suggested to him that he must be the most hissed man in the business, and he agreed. 'What's more,' he added, 'I shall probably be well hissed at close of play.' He has the knack of achieving a love-hate relationship with the children. They boo and hiss as he threatens them with lines like 'I'll send you all back to school', or 'I'll poison your ice-creams in the interval'. But in spite of this and his villainy in the show they always end up feeling sorry for him.

We couldn't let him go without a display of his talent. So he recited Sir Henry Newbolt's famous poem 'There's a breathless hush in the Close tonight. Ten to make and the match to win'. He did it in a Victorian way with full dramatic effect. He followed this with a somewhat lighter rendition – a piece by Norman Gale which he did in his Arlott voice. 'I bowled three curates once with three consecutive balls'. Finally he brought us all into the act as the accompaniment to his performance of a marvellous cricketing parody by A. M. Robertson of the Nightmare Song from Gilbert and Sullivan's *Iolanthe*. All we had to do was to say 'rump-rump-rump' in the background while he sang in a very pleasant light baritone. He had to leave us to go back to London to be Chairman of the Old Time Music Hall at the Players' Theatre – and needless to say we hissed and booed him as he left the box with a blood-curdling shout of 'Silence, you dogs!'.

We had a slight panic at the Lord's Test. Our lunch-time guest failed

No Views from the Boundary today: Brian Johnston, Trevor Bailey and Henry Blofeld taking lunch behind the commentary box at Lord's.

to turn up. Remarkable really, when you consider that he was a certain Mr T. Wogan, who had regularly to get up at 5.30 am every weekday, and always managed to arrive punctually for his early Radio 2 programme. Actually I believe he was late once when he got himself locked into a newly-built bathroom. He did finally turn up at Lord's *after* the lunch interval murmuring something about heavy traffic. However, he let slip that he had been watching the Test on TV so possibly he became so

YORKSHIRE TELEVISION LTD

The cricket commentator who 'went legit' – Michael Charlton.

enthralled that he forgot his appointment with us. We talked to him during intervals in the afternoon, mainly about the Lord's Taverners of which he was President. They had just returned from playing a match at Monte Carlo, which Terry had also attended in his Presidential capacity.

Our lunch-time spot was saved by that inveterate cricket-watcher Robin Bailey, who is invariably to be found on the top balcony of the Lord's pavilion. With author Peter Tinniswood he had been our guest in 1983, when they both related some of the hilarious *Tales from a Long Room*, featuring Robin as the crusty Brigadier. He kindly agreed to help us out and he told us about Peter's new book *The Brigadier in Season*. In it the Pope visits a Test Match, and as is his habit kneels down and kisses the turf on the cricket pitch – thereby leaving a sticky patch at one end. To the obvious delight of 'Blowers' in the box, Robin recalled how the Brigadier had once visited the 'staid old dank Norman pile' of Blofeld Castle in a chapter entitled Blofeld Revisited. Robin was in fact taking a day off from filming a new six-part TV series by Keith Waterhouse. In it he and Michael Aldridge are resurrecting those two cricket-besotted characters Charters and Caldicott – first created by Basil

Radford and Naunton Wayne in the film *The Lady Vanishes*. Indeed at the Old Trafford Test three weeks later there they were filming during play in the pavilion or among the crowd.

We got chatting about actors who love cricket, and top of the list was Trevor Howard. He always had a clause written into his film contracts guaranteeing that there would be no filming during the Lord's Test. Trevor also arranged his overseas filming to fit in with Tests in Australia or the West Indies. Robin said that one winter Trevor's wife, Helen Cherry, had been out shopping and on returning home found a note from Trevor left on the kitchen table. It simply said 'gone to the cricket'. What it did not explain was that the cricket happened to be taking place in Australia. Robin was in Australia during Peter May's tour in 1959 playing Professor Higgins in *My Fair Lady*. I went to the dress rehearsal at Her Majesty's Theatre in Melbourne. I shall never forget it. There was no air-conditioning at the theatre then and the temperature outside was 108 degrees. The house was packed and the heat was unbearable. What it must have been like for the cast I dread to think, as they were all wearing typical English clothing, with the Professor in the famous long cardigan. I've never seen actors sweat more and I felt dreadfully sorry for them. They had been assured by the management that it never got too hot. They begged to differ. Another actor we mentioned was Rex Harrison. I saw him play the part of a professional cricketer at Oxford in the middle Thirties. It was a play called *Mother of Pearl*, starring the French actress Alice Delysia. I shall always remember her wringing her hands in despair because she didn't understand cricket. 'What is all this,' she cried in her broken English, 'about No Balls?'.

With his deep resonant voice Robin has perfected the character of the Brigadier and there must be many retired Colonels in the pavilions of England who recognise themselves when they see him on TV.

At Headingley we were glad to welcome back an old cricket commentator friend – Michael Charlton. Nowadays people associate him with current affairs programmes over here on both TV and Radio. But from the mid-Fifties to early Sixties he was the regular commentator for the Australian Broadcasting Commission at a time when Alan McGilvray was working for commercial radio. Michael was here for the 1956 Australian tour and as one of his highlights remembers Jim Laker's 19 wickets at old Trafford. He said that after the match he went out to inspect the pitch, which the Australian team had so vigorously criticised. He found at the Warwick Road end a small circle about the size of a large plate exactly on a length, on or just outside the off-stump. Jim Laker, who took all his wickets from the Stretford end, had remorselessly and accurately pitched ball after ball on this circular spot.

I asked Michael who he thought was the outstanding captain he had seen playing. Surprisingly, without any hesitation he picked Keith

Miller, who funnily enough never captained Australia. He gave as his reasons for the choice the fact that Keith, though a natural cricketer and as such no great tactician, was an inspirational captain, who commanded great loyalty in his side. Most important too, he was a *lucky* captain who was always prepared to take risks to win. Keith pretended to be more casual than he actually was, and Michael told us a marvellous story about when Keith was captaining New South Wales in a Sheffield Shield match at Newcastle. He led the NSW team out on to the field, striding majestically ahead of them. Jim Burke ran after him and said 'Nugget, we've got 12 men on the field, what shall we do?' Without looking back Keith called over his shoulder 'Well, somebody bugger off then' and continued on his way to the middle.

Michael was different to the usual Australian commentators in that he had something approaching an English accent. He explained that he was born in New Zealand and his Father had taught him not to use 'Colonial twang'. He left cricket commentary to present the Australian equivalent of Panorama called Window on the World. I asked him why he decided to switch his career. He said that when on Richie Benaud's tour of India in 1959–60 he had sat next to Nehru at a dinner and had interviewed him afterwards. He then 'got a taste for it'. It was obvious to me by his remarks in the box and from a letter which he wrote to me afterwards that he sadly missed the fun and camaraderie of the commentary box. Although politics have brought him a very good living in this country, cricket is obviously still his first love.

His outstanding memory will always be the famous Brisbane tie between Australia and West Indies in 1960, where he was one of the commentators. He took us ball by ball through that dramatic last over which started with 6 runs needed by Australia and 3 wickets to fall. Luckily he was not commentating at the time. He says 'luckily' because there was an almighty muddle and at the end many people on the ground did not know the result. There was a blood-red sunset which made it nearly impossible to read the score-board. Not that that mattered much because with all the sensational happenings on the pitch the men working the score-board panicked and got everything wrong. It was not surprising really, with Benaud being caught down the leg-side, Hall missing a chance to run out Meckiff and then colliding with Kanhai in an attempt to catch Grout. Then came the two dramatic run-outs. Grout was out by a foot when going for the winning run – a magnificent throw by Hunte from the mid-wicket boundary. And then finally off the seventh ball Meckiff was run out by Solomon throwing down the stumps from sideways on. No wonder people lost count. Joe Solomon thought the West Indies had won. Frank Worrell thought they had lost, and later described the match to Michael as a 'game for cool fools'. And to cap it all the Australian commentator (let him be nameless) said that the match was a draw! Michael saw Don Bradman watching with a newspaper in his hand. At the end of the over it had been torn to shreds.

So, at least Michael can say that he was there, which is more than some of the Press and one of the commentators can say. Early in the afternoon when the match looked a certain draw they had caught an early plane back to Sydney. They only learned about the tie when they saw the headlines in the Sydney evening paper.

Our welcome guest at Old Trafford was the popular ex-England rugby football captain, Bill Beaumont. He used to be an enthusiastic club cricketer, and has a strong connection with the Lancashire County Cricket Club. He has been a member and keen supporter for many years, and his uncle J. F. Blackledge was made captain of Lancashire for one season in 1962, although, unbelievably, he had never previously played a single game of first-class cricket. Bill's greatest rugby moments were when he captained the North to victory over the All Blacks at Otley in 1979, and when England under his captaincy won the Grand Slam in 1980. In addition he captained the British Lions in South Africa in 1980.

It was interesting to hear him comparing the captaincy of a rugby side with that of a cricket team. In rugby for much of the time Bill had his head tucked down in the middle of the scrum, and yet in such a fast moving game he had to make instant decisions which needed a lot of quick thinking. And when physically tired and running from scrum to scrum, or ruck to ruck, he always had to be thinking of the state of the game and what tactics to employ. In contrast a cricket captain has much more time to think, especially in the field when he can – and sadly often does – slow up the game while he makes field adjustments or bowling changes. Admittedly it does become more difficult when he himself is batting, especially in the fast moving limited-overs games. Then he may have to try to work out complicated run rates whilst trying to concentrate on his own batting.

But Bill felt that he was nearer to his players the whole time and able to communicate to them immediately his wishes or instructions. We have all seen a cricket captain – remote on the pavilion balcony – trying to make understandable signals to his batsmen out in the middle. Bill admitted that a rugby captain has to lead by example for the full 80 minutes. He has to be here, there and everywhere, encouraging his side vocally (if he has any breath left!) over the noise of the crowd. Bill was always in the thick of things and had all these somewhat indefinable qualities which make up a great leader. Only once did he appear to lose control of his team. It was during half-time in the match versus Australia at Twickenham in 1981. He was haranguing his troops as they sucked their oranges, urging them on to even greater efforts in the second half. He suddenly noticed that their attention was wandering. He soon found out why, as he looked up and saw one of the most famous

Derek Nimmo, more soberly dressed than he was at The Oval.

streakers of all time – Erika Roe – running on to the field, carrying all before her. He had to admit that he temporarily forgot about the match.

Bill felt that on a tour abroad a rugby captain has a harder job off the field than his counterpart in cricket. Cricketers in these days of crowded and compressed tours have little spare time to themselves, unless they happen to be the unlucky four or five who don't play in the Tests. But on a rugby tour there are only two matches a week – two hours 40 minutes of play. So the players do have a lot of time to themselves and it's not all that easy for a captain to keep them amused and out of mischief, and their morale up. We were delighted to hear that Bill was definitely *not* in favour of the kissing which has unfortunately become an accepted habit in first-class cricket. In fact we got the impression that Bill rather resented even a pat on the back for anyone who has scored a try. He also compared players' reactions to referees and umpires. In rugby any dissent is immediately punished with a ten-metre penalty and it is very rare for the players to surround a referee in protest as they do in soccer. Alas in cricket, players are more and more ostentatiously showing their displeasure at umpires' decisions, and never seem to receive any reprimand from the umpires or from their captain. I would bet that if Bill was a cricket captain he would immediately stamp on any dissent.

Bill is a large man, strong both in personality and physique. He is quiet with obviously strong principles. A gentle giant – off the field at least! It was not difficult to see why he had made such a magnificent captain. And yet – can you believe it – because he has written a book to make some money for his family he has been classified as a professional and forbidden to give his considerable talents to help coach and encourage young players. How crazy can one get?

Derek Nimmo caused quite a sensation as he passed through the Surrey members on his way up to our commentary box at The Oval. He might almost have come straight off the set of *White Cargo*. He was wearing a white suit with a red carnation in the button-hole, Panama hat, and white shoes. All he lacked was a fly-whisk. I thought he looked splendid but was shocked to see that he was wearing a Kerry Packer tie. He said he had put it on to annoy me and that although he wouldn't have dared to wear it at Lord's, he thought he could get away with it at The Oval. He rightly described it as 'a sort of bastardised MCC tie'.

He told us that he was born in Lancashire, had played cricket at school and had always enjoyed watching it. His father took him to the 1948 Old Trafford Test versus Australia, where he managed to get the autographs of Edrich and Compton. He failed however to get near enough to Bradman to ask him for his. In fact he had to wait till 1979 at Adelaide when he sat next to Sir Donald and plucked up the courage to ask him then. He watches a lot of cricket overseas these days, because he runs a theatrical company which regularly tours the Middle and Far East. In

A life-long Middlesex fan – Barry Norman.

fact in the autumn of 1984 he was going to Hong Kong with the play *There's a Girl in My Soup*. Since he was wearing a silk shirt I asked him if he had got it in Hong Kong. He said yes he had, from a Mr Sam, who also supplied Prince Philip and Prince Charles. After this bit of name-dropping he recalled the small Hong Kong Cricket ground right in the middle of the teeming city. He once saw the Red Bank of China which towered over the ground festooned with Russian flags, and Keith Miller taking pot shots at it by hitting sixes out of the ground.

He had some ancient field glasses slung round his neck and they were bedecked with badges from racecourses all round the world. He admitted that he always tries to be in Australia at the time of the famous Melbourne Cup, and also boasted that he once owned two brood mares. Derek made some rather derogatory remarks about the aircraft trays off which we eat the excellent lunches sent up to us by Cornhill. He had expected cutlery, white table-cloth and damask napkins. However, he seemed to appreciate the meat pie and is the only one of our interviewees who has eaten steadily throughout the session.

He's a versatile chap and claims to have done the first *commercial* Test cricket commentary from Adelaide. However, as he was not allowed to talk while the action was on but had to wait for between the overs, it was not a great success. In view of his great virtuosity in the radio programme Just A Minute, I asked him if he would do 60 seconds on Ian Botham without repeating a word, which is what they have to do. However, he declined, saying he would need an extra fee. He said that the two best players at the game were Kenneth Williams and Clement Freud. He had attended Freud's 60th birthday party in April, and with his tongue in his cheek (I hope) Freud had said in his speech ... 'All my dearest friends in the whole wide world are here tonight – everyone I love the best. There are 17 members of the Liberal Party, and I am the only Liberal here tonight'.

We talked about Derek's tendency to play clerical roles and he said it was probably because he had a pompous voice. He also said it was rather embarrassing because, especially in Australia, people thought he really *was* a clergyman. As a result he was asked to attend bible readings, and once even asked to preach. He also had to be very careful not to swear, and several times shocked people by using the word 'bloody', which is after all very mild for Australia. When he was playing the curate Noot in the TV series All Gas and Gaiters the Archdeacon was played by Robertson Hare. He was in his late eighties and somewhat naturally did not always get his lines right. On one occasion he was meant to ask the bishop 'May I please have a bed for the night?' Instead of this he said 'May I have a *bird* for the night?' In the resulting laughter Robertson Hare was heard muttering to himself 'Oh calamity, thing upon thing'.

He told Derek that in the Great War he was in the bicycle corps. When Derek asked him what happened when they saw the Germans, Robertson Hare replied 'We took cover behind our bicycles'. He was eventually invalided out of the bicycle corps because when jumping on to his bike one day ... 'I landed on my left testicle which assumed enormous proportions'. He was a lovely little man and thoroughly enjoyed a game of cricket, although he was rather short-sighted. In fact I'm afraid he lived up to his nickname of 'Bunny'.

I finally asked Derek about his famous toes which he twiddled nightly for five years during the run of *Charley Boy*. He said they had always been double-jointed and once when rehearsing a play with Moira Lister in Johannesburg they were stuck on how to end a scene. For some reason he had his shoes and socks off and began twiddling his toes. 'That's it,' cried Moira, 'That will bring the curtain down.' And so it was with *Charley Girl*. They wanted him to fill in for a minute or so, and he suddenly remembered his toes. He told us he never got very good notices, but that his toes always stole the show. Well, it was a hot day at The Oval, so we didn't ask Derek to do his toe trick. And he was still tucking into his pie when it was time for us to go back to the studio for the lunch-time cricket scores.

Our sixth and last visitor of the season was the versatile Barry Norman, film critic, presenter, interviewer on both TV and radio, and a novelist with seven books under his belt. He was the only one of the six we interviewed in 'View From The Boundary' in 1984 who still actively plays cricket. When time allows he turns out for his local Hertfordshire village of Datchworth and also represents the Lord's Taverners. In fact, on the day after our interview he was off to play for the Taverners at the beautiful ground at Arundel.

I asked him whether the days of the village blacksmith wearing braces was over so far as village cricket is concerned. He confirmed that it is, and that spotless white flannels are the order of the day. But not so long ago he said he had played against Sir Michael Balam's village and one of their batsmen came in to bat with no collar, brown trousers and black boots and proceeded to hit 50 in 15 minutes. He enjoys playing for the Lord's Taverners because all the ex-Test players who play are his heroes and he has 'never met a cricketer I haven't liked'.

He goes to America a lot for his film programmes and naturally enough to Hollywood. He sadly reported that the great days of Hollywood cricket are no more. There is still cricket played in Los Angeles, mostly by West Indians, but the team of exiled English actors – such as Sir C. Aubrey Smith, Nigel Bruce, Ronald Colman and David Niven – no longer exists. He said that nowadays the film actors seem to prefer 'a bizarre form of rounders'. I couldn't resist asking him what he thought of all the many film stars he meets; what are they really like? He said that they are prettier than the rest of us but certainly not brighter. In fact they are a bit dumb, incredibly egotistical and talk of little except themselves. I asked him to pick out his favourite actress if he had the courage to do so. Well, he had, and without hesitation chose Meryl Streep, giving her full marks for intelligence.

He shudders at being described as a TV personality but accepts that by appearing so often, he is regularly recognised. Most people are very kind but he did overhear the following recently. Two ladies were watching a Lord's Taverners match, and as Barry passed he saw one of them nudge the other. 'Who is he?' she asked in a loud voice. 'Oh', replied her friend, 'he's the one on the telly – the one you can't stand.'

Barry's new novel *Sticky Wicket* had just been published and it is a very funny book. Its hero is a young diffident TV presenter called Andrew Weston for whom everything seems to go wrong. I asked Barry if the character was modelled on himself. 'Not really,' he said, 'but all the things which happen in the book are a projection of all the worst things that have happened to me.' There is one hilarious scene in a TV studio where Andrew is trying to interview a stripper, who mistakenly thinks she is expected to do her act and starts to strip off. In an attempt to stop her Andrew leans forward to try to cover her up, and accidently pulls off her dress, revealing all. She promptly slaps him in the face, accuses him of trying to molest her and chaos reigns in the studio. Barry denied ever actually having had to interview a stripper but wondered 'how he would have handled her' (loud laughter in the commentary box).

Barry has also managed to write very wittily about a cricket match — not an easy thing to do. Needless to say the hero, Andrew, features prominently. Facing an aggressive long-haired fast bowler called The Animal he ducks under the first five bouncers, but when he sees the last ball coming straight at his head he holds his bat horizontally above him as protection. The ball hits the bat and soars over a hedge for six. The Animal is not pleased and later when he comes into bat hits a ball from Andrew straight back at his face. Again, in self-protection, Andrew sticks up a hand, and feels a searing pain in his left buttock as he falls back on to the stumps at the bowler's end. But to the general amazement the ball stays in his hand and an enraged Animal is out. Barry said exactly the same thing happened to him when playing for the Lord's Taverners at Scarborough. He was bowling to Mike Denness who drove back fiercely at him. To protect himself he flung up his right hand and caught an incredible catch. Some of the crowd actually thought he had done it on purpose, and loudly applauded.

And finally, on rather a sad note, I asked him what was his most embarrassing interview. He recalled the occasion when he went out to Milan to interview the late Richard Burton, whom he much liked and admired. He did admit though that when they went out the evening before he could in no way keep up with Richard's drinking tempo. Anyway, the next day he started the interview which went quite well for a few minutes. He then asked a question to which there was no reply from Richard. He put the question again, still receiving no reaction. Suddenly he and his producer heard some gentle snoring and there was Richard, fast asleep. They called out 'Richard, wake up' several times to no avail. So they quickly collected their gear and slipped out of the room.

It was then time to say goodbye to Barry and to wish him luck at Arundel the next day (where I'm sorry to say he pulled a muscle!). As I said at the start, our Saturday lunch-times have been enlivened by every one of our friendly visitors – cricket-lovers all. We have already got one or two lined up for next season, and we all look forward to giving them a warm and hospitable welcome.

The Fifth Test at The Oval
Tony Cozier

And so it came to pass that the West Indies returned 'home', to The Oval, in the heart of London's West Indian community, to create history. No team in all those years of Test cricket had ever beaten England in all five Tests of a series in England and those residents of Brixton and the surrounding districts who will always regard themselves as West Indian, regardless of their citizenship, were prepared for a grand occasion. They were in no doubt about the certainty of what came to be known as 'The Blackwash' – 'Whitewash', in the circumstances, didn't seem quite the appropriate phrase!

England, for a multitude of reasons, had been convincingly beaten in the first four Tests to such an extent that the result of this final match was being taken as read even before a ball was bowled. In such a warm, dry summer even the weather showed no signs of repriving England. Such defeatism overcomes almost every sporting team in similar straits and West Indians, not least Clive Lloyd himself, could readily sympathise with England's plight. When Australia, principally through Lillee and Thomson, inflicted their 5-1 drubbing on the West Indies in Australia in 1975–76, Lloyd was reduced to drifting around the field just as David Gower was now, dejected captains in a state of mesmerised shock.

Those days were long since past for Lloyd, whose team had developed under him into a truly great one. But *the* greatest? Its record merited strong claims in its favour and these were duly advanced throughout the summer, not only by its partisan devotees who were together in their thousands

---

You all know how generous people are in sending us cakes and other sorts of goodies. Last summer during The Oval Test their kindness really went too far. The Egg Marketing Board sent a giant cream cake with an iced cricket match on top. It was delivered to our box by a large yellow chicken. I imagine there was a young lady inside but unfortunately we never saw her. It was a particularly gooey cake and took up a lot of room in the box. So much so that Trevor Bailey accidentally sat on it and covered the seat of his trousers with cream.   **B.J.**

---

during this match to beat their drums, blow their trumpets and shout themselves hoarse. Early in the piece, Richie Benaud had declared, in his usual forthright manner guaranteed to stir the pot of discussion, that he could not imagine a stronger team in the history of the game. During the course of this Test, Jim Laker, who played opposite Benaud in the great Ashes era of the 1950s and who now shares the television commentary box with him, agreed with the former Australian captain's assessment.

Back in the West Indies, my own paper, *The Sunday Sun* of Barbados, was quick to cash in on the debate, inviting readers to nominate their strongest West Indies team of all time from four contenders. They were those of 1950 in England, series winners 3-1, in which the 'Three Ws' and 'those two little pals of mine, Ramadhin and Valentine' were the heroes; 1963 in England under Sir Frank Worrell including Sobers, Kanhai, Hunte, Butcher, Hall, Griffith and Gibbs, also 3-1 winners; 1976, and this present team, both under Lloyd in which fast bowling and positive batting were the cornerstones. Our readers opted for 1963, a choice which coincided with my own, although I have never known a fitter, more dedicated team than the current one. However, there was little in it. Such an exercise, of course, is nothing more than a hypothetical irrelevance since no teams from separate eras can be adequately compared. Yet it made for many hours' argument and, I am sure, increased bar sales as much in the rum shops of Bridgetown and Kingston as in the pubs of Brixton and Kilburn. It certainly increased sales of *The Sunday Sun* – without the expense of running bingo games with exorbitant prizes.

If this 1984 team was, indeed, the greatest of all teams – or even the greatest West Indian team – it was mismatched against opposition which many, including most of my illustrious colleagues in the TMS team, were convinced was the weakest to represent England. To present a worthy challenge, England needed to be able to select from all of its players and, because of the three-year ban on those who undertook the unauthorised South African tour in 1982, Peter May and his panel were unable to do this. West Indians know their cricket and were prepared to accept that some of those debarred would have made a difference to England's ailing cause, notably Graham Gooch whose belligerent attitude to fast bowling had proved so successful in his previous two series against the West Indies. Yet the West Indies had not lost a single Test in England since 1969 and, throughout the summer, I would hear complaints from West Indians about what they saw as attempts to belittle the performances of their team in the Press, on the radio and on television.

Cool it, I would plead with them, remembering how our own media used to get itself into a flap when the West Indies were doing poorly in the past. In the 1970s, for instance, when we went more than 20 Tests with just one victory and lost to India at home, we vilified even Gary Sobers and dropped Lance Gibbs, Roy Fredericks and Clive Lloyd. National sporting defeat can often be regarded as national sporting disgrace and cause strange reactions among the populace. Now the demise of England's cricket was being blamed not only on international politics which had temporarily ostracised Gooch and company but also on the glut of overseas players, unfair tactics by the West Indies fast bowlers who delivered too many bouncers, the groundsmen, the Government, Arthur Scargill, Boy George – you name it. At least no government has yet threatened national cricket teams with jail sentences if they lost as was the case with Liberia's national soccer squad at the African

Nations' Cup some years ago although John Carlisle might well be working up to that in his next private members' bill at Westminster.

By the time we got to The Oval, there were those, I am sure, who might have welcomed such stern methods to deal with England's players and selectors alike. The players had provided the popular press with as much juicy material about their private lives as politicians and pop stars. Reports of shenanigans on their winter tour of New Zealand and Pakistan were followed, during the summer, by a publican's account of late-night goings-on during the Headingley Test. Of the many condemnations of these attitudes none was more strident than that of Ray Illingworth which appeared in the newspapers just prior to the Test although there were others from the TMS box at various stages of the series which seemingly touched nerve ends in the England dressing-room. For their part, the selectors had already chosen 19 players in their futile attempt to find the formula against failure. As many names again had been advanced for their consideration by those who follow the game professionally, day in, day out, for the media.

For this Test, two more were added to England's list. Jon Agnew, the beanpole fast bowler from Leicestershire in the midst of his best season, and the powerful Kent all-rounder Richard Ellison were introduced for their debuts to the exclusion of Norman Cowans and Nick Cook. The West Indies simply replaced Winston Davis with Malcolm Marshall, which was like substituting a Polaris missile with a Cruise, just as lethal but more accurate. Unlucky to have missed the touring team in the first place, Davis was summoned from the ranks of the Glamorgan team at Chelmsford after Marshall's broken thumb and Milton Small's puffy knee reduced Lloyd's options to only four fast bowlers. Lloyd could just as well have asked for Andy Roberts (temporarily helping out Leicestershire), Wayne Daniel, with Middlesex, or Ricardo Ellcock, with Worcestershire. The West Indies' arsenal is at present unlimited and awesome. As it was, Davis had done his job more than adequately at Old Trafford, including a night-watchman's innings of 77. Yet still there was no room for him with the team at full strength, which emphasised another reason for current West Indian strength, the quality of the reserves.

This, then, was the state of affairs as we headed for The Oval, its surrounds jammed, it seemed, with every West Indian in London, pouring forth from the tube station in bright, warm sunshine down the Harleyford Road. For those of us who had not ventured into the ground since the previous season's World Cup, there were sights to behold. The new grandstand to the east of the pavilion, dominated by its plush boxes which take advantage of the affluence of the business world, was snazzy indeed and the seats in the open sections were freshly painted in bright colours, made all the brighter by the morning sunlight. The old girl had had a facelift although it was not yet complete and made her look rather like one of those ageing Hollywood stars who hasn't got the formula for rejuvenation quite right. Next time, maybe.

The surgical work also resulted in a few transplants, notably of the Press box which now found itself no longer ensconced in its cramped quarters adjoining the secretary's office but precariously perched, in the form of a prefab, in the south-western corner of the ground. As I remembered it, this was precisely where the largest and most vociferous of the West Indian supporters had always congregated to drink their Red Stripe beer and Cockspur rum, to lunch on their rice and peas and pig tails and to enjoy their days in traditional fashion – in other words like a carnival. They were indignant about this intrusion. The presence of the Press box was seen, at the very least, as a violation of their territorial integrity. They would not be easily moved, by Press or police, from a spot they had colonised since the earliest days of West Indies Tests at The Oval. Throughout the first day, they engulfed the new, unseemly structure, making life miserable for those inside, and, at the end of it, the Press appeared to be about to surrender. After six hours of unrelenting bombardment from bells, trumpets, impromptu drums and potential town criers, reports in the morning newspapers read like United Nations speeches from ambassadors whose countries were under attack.

Mercifully, compromise was reached, reportedly through the arbitration of the police, and the cheering section moved some way from the relieved representatives of Fleet Street. Not that this meant any reduction in the decibel level. It had been present at all grounds, to a greater or lesser degree, and proved particularly irksome to radio listeners, who wrote in their thousands to complain; to England's batsmen who, at The Oval, found they couldn't continue and to TMS commentators, not least FST whose main grouse apppeared to be not so much the noise itself but its lack of rhythm! In future, we may have to fly a steel band over to replace the dustbin lids and out-of-tune horns. Still, it could have been worse on that first day. West Indian merriment was comparatively muted as England reduced the West Indies to their lowest total of the series, 190, with controlled swing bowling aided by some indisciplined batting. Ian Botham, having announced his decision to rest from the winter tour of India, took 5 wickets, Paul Allott 3 and Ellison, with his big, banana outswingers, 2.

It was left to the venerable captain to prevent further collapse with his undefeated 60. Even though we had heard it more than once in the past, this was obviously going to be his last Test in England and, only a few days earlier, he wasn't sure he would make it. A serious bout of the 'flu laid him low over the weekend, and he was confined to bed and able to eat hardly anything. Antibiotics and his own determination to play allowed him to keep the date but when he put on his blazer in preparation for the toss in the morning, he took it off again thinking he had picked up Joel Garner's by

A wicket for Botham. A bouncer has accounted for Marshall.

mistake. In fact, it was his own and only then did he appreciate how debilitating his illness had been for he had lost several pounds. Yet here he was steadying the team in crisis, batting for almost three and a half hours. No one playing is held in higher regard than Lloyd and the reception he received from the crowd as he walked to the wicket was indicative of this. The crowds rose and applauded him all the way to the middle, a spontaneous action which was enough to bring a lump to the throat of anyone with an ounce of emotion in his soul.

The Oval is a great place for meeting old friends from home, now resident in England, and, as usual, I came across several as I wended my way from commentary to Press box at intervals during the day. 'Don't worry, man' said Fergie Kellman who used to bowl leg-breaks when we were at Lodge School in Barbados together many moons ago, but who has long since been resident in Thornton Heath. 'If we make 20, they'll make 19!' Funny, I said, I'd just heard the same theory advanced, if not quite so bluntly, by one Trevor Bailey on TMS. Fergie and Trevor proved correct. England's batsmen were again found wanting and fell 28 short, leaving the match a second innings contest. And a contest it proved to be for it was not until Desmond Haynes and Jeffrey Dujon put on 82 for the fifth wicket midway through Saturday afternoon that the West Indies took a firm hold of the match. After that, the lead became progressively more out of England's reach and, as had been the case in most of the earlier Tests, it was only a matter of time over the final two days.

It was a particularly happy Saturday for Haynes, the happiest of cricketers. He wears a gold chain around his neck – well, one of several – with the words 'Live, Love, Laugh' inscribed on it. Others may wear their zodiac signs but none reveals the character of the individual more accurately than Haynes' proclamation. In seven previous innings in the series he had passed 20 only once and kept his place mainly because the third opener, Richie Richardson, was off form as well. Yet he remained, throughout, as cheerful as ever, the clown in the team coach, a real livewire, always full value as a team man. Now, at the very last time of asking, the pressure was on him, in more ways than one, Only a few days before, his mother had arrived, along with his two brothers, on her very first trip outside Barbados. They had come along with a team Haynes had personally organised from his area in Barbados, called the Cavaliers, on a tour of England which Haynes had set up. The night before the Test, the Cavaliers assembled for a few drinks with their leader at the West Indies' hotel in Russell Square. Only half in jest, they advised him that if he didn't get runs in this match, he might find himself dropped from his own team which had no room for out-of-form batsmen! So Desmond had to come good and that Saturday night there was a lot of living and laughing and, possibly, loving as well!

As far as TMS's representative was concerned, it was early to bed. Next day, a Press team was scheduled to play against Texaco who had sponsored the one-day internationals at the start of the summer and who had looked after us so lavishly. Apparently, they wanted to find out if we could actually play the game about which we write so critically. Shrewd skipper that he is, the *Daily Mail*'s Brian Scovell saw to it that he braced our team with a couple of ringers just in case things went wrong and, since one happened to be B. S. Chandrasekhar and since I had informed him I would keep wicket, I thought it advisable to go into action with a clear head. Chandra's leg-breaks and googlies would confuse me enough without having to cope with rum-induced cobwebs as well. As it turned out, the 'keeping was efficiency itself, not only to Chandra but to the other ringer, Sarfraz Nawaz, as well; we won and Texaco entertained us wonderfully just the same.

On the grounds that I would be stiff and sore following my ordeal bending behind the timbers, I managed to pass off my scheduled Monday morning stint for Radio 4's Today programme to Henry Blofeld, as ever a friend indeed despite his many commitments to stations in the Australian outback, the Papua New Guinea highlands, the Indian Himalayas and the Russian steppes. If the truth be known, I had been terrified of this assignment since the Lord's Test. We draw lots to determine who fills the morning call, which necessitates getting to the ground at 8.00 am, and, at Lord's, mine was for the Monday. When I duly arrived at the car park entrance to perform my duty for the BBC that fateful morning I discovered that, in the rush, I had forgotten my pass. It was, at first, only cause for a mild flutter of concern since, as anyone who has had any dealings with them knows, gatemen the world over are reasonable, understanding men.

'I'm afraid I've left my pass back at the hotel but I'm only here for a short report for BBC radio and will be right back.' At eight in the morning I thought the explanation and the request reasonable enough. Not to the Lord's custodian it wasn't and it might have been easier to try getting through a miners' picket line. Suddenly, therefore, I found myself in a panic, the image of a scowling Peter Baxter before me, demanding to know why I hadn't showed for my assignment. In the end, the car park attendant, who had overheard my pleas to the uncompromising gateman, offered the suggestion that I pay the £4.50 car park fee which would allow me into the ground. Day saved, Radio 4's Today report given, all 45 seconds of it, and Cozier £4.50 out of pocket. Was it all worth it, I wonder.

With the Tests often finishing a day early, the one who drew the morning report for the last day could usually expect a lie-in. This time, however, the match did go into the fifth day even though the result was, by then, a foregone conclusion. Botham was still there, 32 not out, along with Downton, with 224 needed by England and, after Headingley 1981, some morning newspapers reminded us that anything was possible. Not this time. England's Superman did have a thrash for a half-hour before he was caught at fine leg hooking and, within another half an hour, just after noon, the West Indies had completed their fifth straight victory, a phenomenal achievement.

Overcome with joy, the West Indian cheering section, which had waited all summer for this moment, could not contain itself and, unwittingly but no less certainly, spoiled what should have been a cherished moment for Lloyd and his peerless team. Instead of being able to walk off the field for the last time with pride and dignity following their triumph, they were forced to flee as if for their lives to the sanctuary of the pavilion, pursued by frenzied fans. Agnew, England's last man, had his bat, gloves and helmet snatched and the West Indian fielders looked more like rugby forwards on the run than cricketers. There was sheer chaos as Ray Illingworth named Haynes 'Man of the Match' and Gordon Greenidge 'Man of the Series' amidst the throng in front of the pavilion which had already breached the inadequate police line. Large doses of Thunderbird wine were forcibly administered to David Gower by an immense lady from the Caribbean, several of the players kept their distance and what had been planned as an impressive ceremony to mark the end of the series had degenerated into a fish-market fracas.

'I'm afraid our Brixtonian friends became a little too enthusiastic and spoiled a great occasion', Clive Lloyd commented in obvious disappointment. These were sentiments which we could all share but it is impossible to adequately convey just what the success of a West Indies cricket team means to those West Indians who now make England their home. Attempting to find out, BBC TV's Sixty Minutes despatched a crew to The Oval. One burly advocate of the theory that Clive Lloyd, Vivian Richards, Gordon Greenidge and the others should be deified was asked to express his feelings about a West Indies Test at The Oval. 'You see my woman', he replied. 'She's my number one. But for this week, cricket is number one and she has to be number two.'

WEST INDIES 1st INNINGS v. ENGLAND (5th TEST) AT KENNINGTON OVAL, LONDON, ON 9,10,11,13,14 AUGUST, 1984.

IN	OUT	MINS	No.	BATSMAN	HOW OUT	BOWLER	RUNS	WKT	TOTAL	6s	4s	BALLS	NOTES ON DISMISSAL Toss: WEST INDIES
11.00	12.17	77	1	C.G.GREENIDGE	LBW	BOTHAM	22	2	45	.	3	51	Pushed across line - ball angled in.
11.00	11.33	33	2	D.L.HAYNES	BOWLED	ALLOTT	10	1	19	.	1	22	Drove across full-length ball. Middle and off stumps hit.
11.35	12.57	82	3	H.A.GOMES	C BOTHAM	ELLISON	18	3	64	.	1	57	Edged drive to 2nd slip - high, two-handed catch.
12.19	1.41	42	4	I.V.A.RICHARDS	C ALLOTT	BOTHAM	8	4	64	.	1	25	Hooked off-stump bouncer high to finer long-leg - running catch.
12.59	1.53	14	5	P.J.DUJON †	C TAVARÉ	BOTHAM	3	5	67	.	.	10	BOTHAM'S 300th TEST WICKET. Gloved bouncer to 1st slip.
1.43	(5.25)	202	6	C.H.LLOYD *	NOT OUT		60			.	5	112	Became 6th highest scorer, passing GS Chappell, when 48. (Tests).
1.55	1.59	4	7	M.D.MARSHALL	C GOWER	ELLISON	0	6	70	.	.	4	Edged drive at outswinger high to 3rd slip (two-handed catch).
2.01	3.14	73	8	E.A.E.BAPTISTE	C FOWLER	ALLOTT	32	7	124	.	5	58	Drove widish ball low to cover.
3.16	4.37	61	9	R.A.HARPER	BOWLED	BOTHAM	18	8	154	.	3	46	Drove across inswinging yorker.
4.39	4.40	1	10	M.A.HOLDING	LBW	BOTHAM	0	9	154	.	.	2	Drove across late inswinger. Botham 5 wkts for 23rd time in Tests.
4.42	4.42	.	11	J.GARNER	C DOWNTON	ALLOTT	6	10	190	.	.	34	Edged off-drive to 'keeper.

* CAPTAIN   † WICKET-KEEPER

EXTRAS	b 1 lb 4 w 7 nb 1	13	0s 19s 421 balls (including 1 no ball)

TOTAL (70 OVERS, 325 MINUTES) **190** all out at 5.25pm on 1st day.

12 OVERS 5 BALLS/HOUR
2.71 RUNS/OVER
45 RUNS/100 BALLS

BOWLER	O	M	R	W	wd/nb	HRS	OVERS	RUNS
AGNEW	12	3	46	0	1/3	1	13	37
ALLOTT	17	7	25	3	-	2	13	27
BOTHAM	23	8	72	5	-/3	3	12	29
ELLISON	18	3	34	2	4/1	4	14	43
						5	13	38
			13					
	70	21	190	10				

RUNS	MINS	OVERS	LAST 50 (in mins)
50	94	20.0	94
100	181	38.5	87
150	267	58.1	86

LUNCH: 64-3 (26 OVERS / 120 MIN.) RICHARDS 8* (61') DUJON 0* (1')

TEA: 136-7 (52 OVERS / 240 MIN.) LLOYD 24* (117') HARPER 8* (24')

WKT	PARTNERSHIP		RUNS	MINS
1st	Greenidge	Haynes	19	33
2nd	Greenidge	Gomes	26	42
3rd	Gomes	Richards	19	38
4th	Richards	Dujon	0	2
5th	Dujon	Lloyd	3	9
6th	Lloyd	Marshall	3	4
7th	Lloyd	Baptiste	54	73
8th	Lloyd	Harper	30	61
9th	Lloyd	Holding	0	1
10th	Lloyd	Garner	36	43

190

Compiled by BILL FRINDALL

ENGLAND 1ST INNINGS — IN REPLY TO WEST INDIES 190 ALL OUT

IN	OUT	MINS	No.	BATSMAN	HOW OUT	BOWLER	RUNS	WKT	TOTAL	6s	4s	BALLS	NOTES ON DISMISSAL
5·38 / 2·17	11·32 / 2·57	92	1	G. FOWLER	C* RICHARDS	BAPTISTE	31	(1) / 7	21 / 116	·	2	61	Retired hurt when 12* - hit on right forearm by lifting ball from Marshall. Edged drive to 2nd slip - sharp chance well taken two-handed.
5·38	5·57	19	2	B.C. BROAD	BOWLED	GARNER	4	1	10	·	·	13	Beaten by superb ball - pitched leg, hit middle & off.
5·59	11·43	42	3	P.I. POCOCK	C* GREENIDGE	MARSHALL	0	2	22	·	·	21	Unable to avoid fast bouncer - simple catch to 4th slip (bat handle)
11·34	1·49	92	4	C.J. TAVARÉ	C* DUJON	HOLDING	16	4	64	·	2	55	Followed quicker, sharply lifting, leg side ball.
11·45	12·26	41	5	D.I. GOWER *	C* DUJON	HOLDING	12	3	45	·	2	34	Failed to avoid bouncer that cut back - off gloves.
12·28	2·19	67	6	A.J. LAMB	LBW	MARSHALL	12	6	84	·	·	40	Beaten by fast ball that cut back and kept low.
1·52	2·14	22	7	I.T. BOTHAM	C* DUJON	MARSHALL	14	5	83	·	1	20	Unable to avoid fast bouncer that glanced gloves.
2·21	3·36	75	8	P.R. DOWNTON †	C* LLOYD	GARNER	16	8	133	·	·	62	Failed to evade fast lifting ball - off gloves to 1st slip.
2·59	(5·35)	77	9	R.M. ELLISON	NOT OUT		20			·	2	43	
3·38	5·27	29	10	P.J.W. ALLOTT	BOWLED	MARSHALL	16	9	156	·	1	24	Off stumps - played back to full length ball - first after resumption.
5·29	5·35	6	11	J.P. AGNEW	BOWLED	MARSHALL	5	10	162	·	·	10	Played on via pads.

* CAPTAIN   † WICKET-KEEPER   **EXTRAS** b 2 lb 4 w - nb 10   **16**   6s 10s 383 balls (including 12 no balls)

TOTAL (61·5 overs, 292 minutes) **162** all out at 5.35pm on 2nd day.

13 OVERS 1 BALLS/HOUR
2.62 RUNS/OVER
42 RUNS/100 BALLS

BOWLER	O	M	R	W	nb		HRS	OVERS	RUNS		RUNS	MINS	OVERS	LAST 50 (in mins)
GARNER	18	6	37	2	5	1	12	22		50	119	25	119
MARSHALL	17·5	5	35	5	5	2	13	28		100	192	39·1	73
HOLDING	13	2	55	2	2	3	11	34		150	272	57·3	80
BAPTISTE	12	4	19	1	·	4	14	43					
HARPER	1	1	0	0	·								
			16										
	61·5	18	162	10									

STUMPS: 10-1 | 5 OVERS / 22 MIN. | FOWLER 4* (22') POCOCK 0* (1')
LUNCH: 57-3 | 27 OVERS / 129 MIN [TAKEN AT 12.50pm - 1st day] | TAVARÉ 15* (75') LAMB 4* (21')
TEA: 133-8 | 54 OVERS / 259 MIN | ELLISON 12* (43') ALLOTT 0* (4')

MARSHALL took five wickets in an innings for the seventh time in his last 10 Tests

WEST INDIES 28 RUNS AHEAD ON FIRST INNINGS

WKT	PARTNERSHIP		RUNS	MINS
1st	Fowler	Broad	10	19
2nd	Fowler / Tavaré	Pocock	11* / 9	31 / 9
3rd	Tavaré	Gower	23	41
4th	Tavaré	Lamb	19	38
5th	Lamb	Botham	19	22
6th	Lamb	Fowler	1	2
7th	Fowler	Downton	32	36
8th	Downton	Ellison	17	37
9th	Ellison	Allott	23	29
10th	Ellison	Agnew	6	6
			162	

Compiled by BILL FRINDALL

WEST INDIES 2ND INNINGS — 28 RUNS AHEAD ON FIRST INNINGS

IN	OUT	MINS	No.	BATSMAN	HOW OUT	BOWLER	RUNS	WKT	TOTAL	6s	4s	BALLS	NOTES ON DISMISSAL
5·46	11·35	51	1	C.G. GREENIDGE	C* BOTHAM	AGNEW	34	1	51	·	4	39	Short ball, cut back sharply - attempted cut steered to 2nd slip
5·46	11·59	436	2	D.L. HAYNES	BOWLED	BOTHAM	125	9	329	·	17	269	7th in Tests; (1st of tour). Played on - aimed off-drive at inswinger.
11·37	11·42	5	3	H.A. GOMES	C* TAVARÉ	ELLISON	1	2	52	·	·	6	Edged drive low to 1st slip - Ellison's first ball of the innings.
11·45	11·58	13	4	I.V.A. RICHARDS	LBW	AGNEW	15	3	69	·	2	11	Played back and across sharp breakback.
12·00	2·28	108	5	C.H. LLOYD *	C* DOWNTON	ELLISON	36	4	132	·	3	62	Edged cut - diving catch in front of 1st slip.
2·30	4·09	77	6	P.J. DUJON †	C* LAMB	ELLISON	49	5	214	·	8	63	Edged drive at outswinger to 1st slip.
4·11	5·21	70	7	E.A.E. BAPTISTE	C* DOWNTON	ALLOTT	5	6	237	·	·	47	Edged offside push to 'keeper.
5·23	5·50	27	8	M.D. MARSHALL	C* LAMB	BOTHAM	12	7	264	·	2	14	Hooked bouncer straight to deep square-leg.
5·52	11·19	30	9	R.A. HARPER	C* DOWNTON	ALLOTT	17	8	293	1	2	17	Played back - inside edge driving - low, 2-handed to left.
11·21	11·19	58	10	M.A. HOLDING	LBW	BOTHAM	30	10	346	1	3	36	Plumb - played back to yorker.
12·01	(12·19)	18	11	J. GARNER	NOT OUT		10			·	1	15	

* CAPTAIN   † WICKET-KEEPER   **EXTRAS** b - lb 12 w - nb -   **12**   2s 42s 579 balls (0 no balls)

TOTAL (96·3 overs, 456 minutes) **346** all out at 12.19pm on 4th day.

12 OVERS 4 BALLS/HOUR
3.59 RUNS/OVER
60 RUNS/100 BALLS

BOWLER	O	M	R	W	nb		HRS	OVERS	RUNS		RUNS	MINS	OVERS	LAST 50 (in mins)
BOTHAM	22·3	2	103	3		1	12	52		50	49	10·5	49
ALLOTT	26	1	96	2		2	13	38		100	137	28·1	88
POCOCK	8	3	24	0		3	13	42		150	199	41·0	62
AGNEW	14	1	51	2		4	14	59		200	248	53·3	49
ELLISON	26	7	60	3		5	12	34		250	352	74·1	104
			12			6	12	31		300	408	86·0	56
	96·3	14	346	10		7	13	53					

STUMPS: 15-0 (2ND DAY) (43 AHEAD) | 4 OVERS / 16 MINUTES | GREENIDGE 10* HAYNES 4*
LUNCH: 98-3 (126 AHEAD) | 28 OVERS / 136 MINUTES | HAYNES 28* (136') LLOYD 19* (60')
TEA: 212-4 (240 AHEAD) | 55 OVERS / 256 MINUTES | HAYNES 76* (256') DUJON 48* (70')
STUMPS: 284-7 (3RD DAY) (312 AHEAD) | 79 OVERS / 377 MINUTES | HAYNES 111* (377') HARPER 14* (11')

WKT	PARTNERSHIP		RUNS	MINS
1st	Greenidge	Haynes	51	51
2nd	Haynes	Gomes	1	5
3rd	Haynes	Richards	17	13
4th	Haynes	Lloyd	63	108
5th	Haynes	Dujon	82	77
6th	Haynes	Baptiste	23	70
7th	Haynes	Marshall	27	27
8th	Haynes	Harper	29	30
9th	Haynes	Holding	36	38
10th	Holding	Garner	17	18
			346	

2ND NEW BALL taken at 11·27am on 4th day
- WEST INDIES 295-8 after 85 overs

Compiled by BILL FRINDALL

ENGLAND 2ND INNINGS   REQUIRING 375 RUNS IN A MINIMUM OF 629 MINUTES

IN	OUT	MINS	No.	BATSMAN	HOW OUT	BOWLER	RUNS	WKT	TOTAL	6s	4s	BALLS	NOTES ON DISMISSAL
12.31	1.47	37	1	G. FOWLER	C' RICHARDS	MARSHALL	7	1	15	·	1	30	Edged fast ball, angled across, to 2nd slip.
12.31	4.17	167	2	B.C. BROAD	C' GREENIDGE	HOLDING	39	2	75	·	·	104	Unable to avoid faster lifter off long run - off glove to gully.
1.49	5.30	201	3	C.J. TAVARÉ	C' RICHARDS	GARNER	49	5	135	·	4	153	(HS · WI) Edged off drive to 2nd slip - fast two-handed catch.
4.19	4.39	20	4	D.I. GOWER *	LBW	HOLDING	7	3	88	·	1	12	Beaten by late inswing - quicker ball off longer run.
4.41	4.44	3	5	A.J. LAMB	C' HAYNES	HOLDING	1	4	90	·	·	2	Fended short ball to right of short leg - longer run.
4.46	11.25	100	6	I.T. BOTHAM	C' MARSHALL	GARNER	54	6	181	·	6	51	50 off 49 balls. Skied hook to deep fine-leg.
5.32	11.37	66	7	P.R. DOWNTON†	LBW	GARNER	10	7	186	·	1	46	Played back - beaten by break back.
11.27	12.01	34	8	R.M. ELLISON	C' HOLDING	GARNER	13	10	202	·	1	24	Edged back foot force at lifting ball to gully.
11.39	11.52	13	9	P.J.W. ALLOTT	C' LLOYD	HOLDING	4	8	200	·	1	6	Edged off-side ball to 1st slip - not in line.
11.54	11.55	1	10	P.I. POCOCK	C' AND BOWLED	HOLDING	0	9	200	·	·	2	'PAIR' - second in successive Tests. Reaction catch - firm drive.
11.57	(12.01)	4	11	J.P. AGNEW	NOT OUT		2			·	·	2	

* CAPTAIN † WICKET-KEEPER

EXTRAS   b -   lb 2   w 1   nb 13   16   0s 15s 432 balls (inc. 14 no balls)

TOTAL   (69.4 OVERS, 332 MINUTES)   202 all out at 12.01 pm

12 OVERS 3 BALLS/HOUR
2.90   RUNS/OVER
47   RUNS/100 BALLS

BOWLER	O	M	R	W		HRS	OVERS	RUNS
MARSHALL	22	5	71	1	1/-	1	13	24
GARNER	18.4	3	51	4	7/-	2	11	32
HOLDING	13	2	43	5	5/1	3	16	27
BAPTISTE	8	3	11	0	1/-	4	11	51
HARPER	8	5	10	0	·	5	13	48
			16	10				
	69.4	18	202	10				

RUNS	MINS	OVERS	LAST 50 (in mins)
50	105	21.5	105
100	205	44.2	100
150	265	56.3	60
200	321	68.0	56

LUNCH: 15-0 | 7 OVERS, 31 MINUTES | FOWLER 7*, BROAD 7*
TEA: 71-1 | 34 OVERS, 152 MINUTES | BROAD 38*(62), TAVARÉ 19*(41)
STUMPS: 151-5 | 58 OVERS, 271 MINUTES | BOTHAM 32*(15), DOWNTON 2*(26)

WEST INDIES WON BY 172 RUNS

MAN OF THE MATCH: D.L. HAYNES

PLAYER OF THE SERIES: C.G. GREENIDGE
(Adjudicator - both awards - R. ILLINGWORTH)

TOTAL TIME LOST : 1 HOUR 1 MINUTE

WKT	PARTNERSHIP		RUNS	MINS
1st	Fowler	Broad	15	37
2nd	Broad	Tavaré	60	128
3rd	Tavaré	Gower	13	20
4th	Tavaré	Lamb	2	3
5th	Tavaré	Botham	45	44
6th	Botham	Downton	46	54
7th	Downton	Ellison	5	10
8th	Ellison	Allott	14	13
9th	Ellison	Pocock	0	1
10th	Ellison	Agnew	2	4

202

Compiled by BILL FRINDALL

ENGLAND v WEST INDIES 1984
Statistical Highlights   Bill Frindall

First Test – Edgbaston

Andy Lloyd, from Oswestry, was only the second Shropshire-born cricketer to represent England and the first to do so in a home Test. He followed W. Newham, the Shrewsbury-born Sussex batsman, whose sole Test appearance was at Sydney in 1887–88.

The West Indies total of 606 was the highest against England since 1976 when Clive Lloyd's side amassed 687 for 8 declared at The Oval.

Viv Richards scored his 5,000th run in Tests when his total reached 13. Only D. G. Bradman (11) among visiting batsmen has exceeded Richards' five Test 100s in England.

The partnership of 150 by Eldine Baptiste and Michael Holding was a ninth-wicket record for West Indies against England.

England suffered only their second defeat in 22 Tests against all countries at Edgbaston – Australia inflicting the first in 1975.

Second Test – Lord's

Lord's celebrated its centenary of Test cricket by staging its 76th official Test to equal the record held by the Melbourne Cricket Ground.

England's opening partnership of Graeme Fowler and Chris Broad was their seventh different pairing in the last eight Tests.

Clive Lloyd (7,000 runs), Ian Botham and Gordon Greenidge (4,000 runs), and Larry Gomes (2,000 runs) achieved notable Test career milestones.

Gordon Greenidge registered the first double century for West Indies at Lord's. His unbroken partnership of 287 with Larry Gomes was a second-wicket record for either country in this series.

The West Indies total of 344 for 1 was the fifth highest in a fourth innings to win a Test match. They lost a second innings wicket for the first time in seven Tests. England had not lost after declaring their second innings since 1948 when Australia scored their famous 404 for 3 at Headingley.

Ian Botham became the first bowler to take 8 wickets against West Indies in a Test in England.

The umpires (Barrie Meyer 7, David Evans 5), equalled the Test record of 12 lbw decisions set in the New Zealand v West Indies Test at Dunedin in 1979–80.

Third Test – Headingley
Michael Holding took his 200th Test wicket when he dismissed Pringle. He was the fourth West Indies bowler to reach this total after L. R. Gibbs, G. St A. Sobers and A. M. E. Roberts.

Bob Willis, in his final Test, extended his world Test record of 'not out' innings to 55 and his record number of wickets by an England bowler to 325.

Only once previously, against Australia in 1921, had England lost the first three Tests of a home series.

Fourth Test – Old Trafford
Old Trafford, like Lord's, celebrated its centenary of Test cricket.

Pat Pocock returned to Test cricket eight years after making the last of his previous 17 appearances. That match, only his third Test at home, was also at Old Trafford and against the West Indies. During his absence England played 86 Tests.

Gordon Greenidge (223) became the first West Indian to score a double century at Old Trafford and the second after Richards in 1976 to reach 200 twice in the same series against any country.

Allan Lamb scored his third 100 in successive Test Matches – the first such instance for England since G. Boycott recorded centuries against Australia at Adelaide in 1970–71 and against Pakistan at Lord's and Headingley in 1971. The last England batsman to score three successive 100s in the same series was K. F. Barrington against Pakistan in 1967.

Fifth Test – The Oval
Ian Botham became the fifth bowler after F. S. Trueman, L. R. Gibbs, D. K. Lillee and R. G. D. Willis to take 300 wickets in Test Matches.

Malcolm Marshall took 5 wickets in an innings for the seventh time in his last ten Tests. In four series crammed into 18 months he has taken 99 wickets at 20.53 runs apiece in only 19 Tests.

Pat Pocock became the second England player after Robert Peel (v Australia in 1894–95) to be dismissed for a pair twice in successive Tests.

West Indies equalled the world record of eight consecutive Test victories set by Australia against England in 1920–21 and 1921. They became the fifth side to win every Test in a five-match rubber, emulating F. M. Worrell's 1961–62 team's drubbing of India. Only one of their last 38 Tests ended in defeat and they extended their undefeated run to 23 matches – the third-longest sequence.

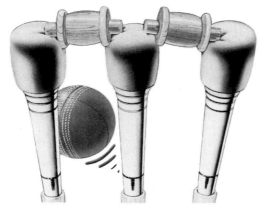

THE SRI LANKANS
AT LORD'S

—————— Tony Lewis——————

This was Sri Lanka's first Test Match in England, and, of course, to play it at Lord's meant a milestone of fruition and maturity for the country which was only 11 Tests old. That they played so magnificently to get the better of a draw is now history. If I relished anything in the commentary box it was the underestimation of the Sri Lankans by Fred Trueman and Trevor Bailey.

Fred said that he thought Paul Allott was not being bowled by Gower because his place on the winter tour to India was safe and that Gower was probably giving others a chance. (Sri Lanka were about to score 491 for 7 in their first innings over two days and 90 minutes!) Trevor suggested before the match that we were about to watch the worst collection of 22 cricketers ever assembled for a Test Match. He later conceded that Sri Lanka could bat. I was amused because I had led two MCC tours to Ceylon in 1970 and 1973, in the days when they were building up steadily to Test Match status. I had seen how strongly they batted. I had sweated with my bowlers at the Colombo Oval trying to prise the ever so correct and durable Sri Lankans out. I could not expect Trevor and Fred to know as much, but I was delighted to see their views change during the five days. Their expert eyes did not miss the quality of technique nor the range of stroke play among the batsmen.

In the Test Match Special box with us was a Sri Lankan who now lives in exile in Sydney, Australia, Gamini Goonesena, once a fine leg-spin and googly bowler for Cambridge University, Notts and Ceylon. Gammy had a tricky time at Lord's, balancing his social performance with the requirements of the summarisers' rota in the box. His return to this country after long absence brought his long-denied disciples out of hiding, demanding a sight, a touch and few words from the great man. Fred Trueman, tired of looking around the box for Gammy, next on the air, kept groaning 'Where's that phantom tea-planter gone now?' When provocatively asked if he remembered playing against Gammy at Fenners or Trent Bridge, Fred said that he only recalled a little black head on its knees behind the bat-handle, praying! How a head kneels you will have to work out for yourself.

Brian Johnston immediately confused everyone with several pronunciations of the same Sri Lankan name. He rejoiced when it was announced that of the 12 Sri Lankans on the score-card, Samaranayake would be left out and John included. Easy. That was until we requested a Sri Lankan reserve player to help with the identification and Brian had to turn to 'our good friend here, who has come up to the box from the dressing-room to help us with the recognising of his colleagues, now, after three days, we've got their names.' And turning to the helper said. 'Now your name is Anusha Samar ... oh! no!'

During the Sri Lankan Test we invited Cabinet Minister Mr Dessanayake to broadcast a short message back home to Sri Lanka in their own Sinhala language. We all listened spellbound to the spate of unintelligible words, nobody understanding a thing. When he had finished I couldn't resist saying, 'Thank you very much, Minister. I couldn't have put it better myself'. He took it very well.   **B.J.**

The start of the match was surprising. David Gower won the toss and put Sri Lanka in to bat on a pitch which had no serious growth of grass on a roaring, sunny day. He said after Sri Lanka's mammoth first innings that he thought the ball would have swung. For optimism unsupported by facts this rivalled Bob Willis's decision to put in Australia at Adelaide. I have never heard of sunshine and heat alone recommending an 'insertion'. Oppressiveness; heavy atmosphere; seaside conditions and others, perhaps, but in too many cases, the decision to put in to bat purely for swing-bowling proves wrong.

On this occasion the ball did not swing for long and Sidath Wettimuny played the innings of a lifetime, 190, and a model for young boys to copy. Trevor and Fred firmly pointed out the merits of his technique and we all observed that he had rolled back the years a couple of decades. He played a

Gamini Goonesena in his playing days at Cambridge.

long innings, for two days, but it never lost its aesthetic appeal. He played the game sideways; he moved right back when he was back, and right forward when he was forward. Simple ancient truths, not followed by the bulk of England players these days.

To find the quality and the spirit of Sri Lankan cricket you must look to the colleges, the most famous of which are Royal and St Thomas's. Gammy Goonesena described for the listeners the crowds of 10,000 who attend the annual dust-up called the Royal-Thomian, Battle of the Blues. It is over 100 years old. So you might guess that Sri Lankan cricket is based on college disciplines too. Players are always perfectly turned out, shoes whitened, flannels pressed. Their sportsmanship is firmly rooted in the best of the Old Boy morality. It was not surprising in this Test Match to hear that they had addressed the umpires David Evans and Dickie Bird as 'Sir'. Sadly, it was also no surprise to learn that the umpires had to talk to Gower, the England captain, in order to check the flow of bad language coming from some of the England side.

Wettimuny's performance must have been received with great joy in Sri Lanka as we talked them through it ball-by-ball. Then came Ranatunga, now an old man of 20! He was strong and much more controlled in his choice of strokes than when I last saw him in Sri Lanka's inaugural Test in Colombo in 1982. He got 84 putting on 148 with Wettimuny.

I always pay a daily visit to the Umpires' Room at a Test Match to say good morning and to have a chat. Dickie Bird never fails to provoke a laugh. I usually tell him there's a deep depression approaching from the southwest and that will mean he will have to make a lot of difficult decisions about the light. This gets him into a terrible state of agitation as it's something he always dreads. However, at the Sri Lankan Test at Lord's he had two other matters on his mind. He was perspiring in the heat because he had to shut the window to keep out the night-watch-man's cat, which at night-time occupied the room. Dickie is allergic to cats and didn't see why the cat should be there during the day. He was also worried because he had just had a letter to say that one of the peacocks at his home in Barnsley had just laid an egg!   **B.J.**

The major virtuoso performance was still to come. The captain, Duleep Mendis, a short man of ample girth and powerful forearms played an innings which is unforgettable for its wide range of strokes and improvisation. If I had to recall one particular shot, it was a hook off Botham's bowling. Mendis was in position quickly, he began the hook but found that the ball had bounced a little higher than he had gauged. Then with a regal flip of the wrists he adjusted to bring the meat of the bat smack against the centre of the ball, firing it like a bullet into the Mound Stand.

Wettimuny and Mendis put on 150, Mendis's share 111. Maybe just to prove that his skill is no fluke he repeated the treatment of England's bowlers in the second innings. Before this match he had already scored a century in each innings of a Test against India. He came alarmingly close this time, too, scoring 95 the second time around.

The England compensations were few but of them Allan Lamb's century must be mentioned. It was his fourth century of the summer and underlines the need to persevere with a player who has the talent even when he has a bad patch. His winter form was awful. However, the three centuries against the West Indies fast bowling must rank as one of the finest series ever by an England batsman. If this last one against less formidable bowling on a perfect pitch was less difficult to achieve, it still remained England's only piece of authority in the five days' play.

Towards the end of the match Neil Chanmugan, the Sri Lankan tour manager, came up into the commentary box to join our ball-by-ball descriptions. Neil was a fine cricketer, hard and competitive and, with others I played against in the early Seventies like Michael Tissera and Anura Tennakoon, prepared the way for Test acceptance by their own high standards. Nor is he a stranger to the microphone because in Sri Lanka he broadcast on the inaugural Test for his island's station.

His thoughts at Lord's were these. 'I hope that our example has stimulated Sri Lankan businessmen. We need sponsorship both for players and for matches. I imagine that the way ahead for us now that we are accepted as decent cricketers is to set up a semi-professional life for our best players ... retained by businesses perhaps but free to play cricket at the top level.

'Also we need advertising support to bring monies into the game. Our country does have rich natural resources and plenty of trading activity, and our cricket is now on TV.'

Sri Lanka is 270 miles long, north to south, and 140 miles across at its widest. There are 14 million inhabitants, mostly Sinhalese. It is a tea and rubber island. You can drive through rice-fields and still hunt leopard. Beaches are delightful but filling up with instant hotels and tourists. Sri Lanka is green, almost smothered by tea estates and palm trees and, astonishingly, it boasts a 90 per cent literacy figure.

However, most of the competitive cricket is played by clubs in Colombo. There is a new four-day match competition to prepare youngsters for the skills and tempo of Test cricket. Yet the miracle of their first Test at Lord's is that they more than held the best that Britain can offer and it is likely that their strong emphasis on college cricket will soon see them beating England for the first time.

It's as easy as that. Duleep Mendis hooks Botham for 6 and Gower can only admire.

SRI LANKA 1st INNINGS v. ENGLAND (Only Test) at LORD'S, LONDON on 23, 24, 25, 27, 28 AUGUST, 1984.

IN	OUT	MINS	No.	BATSMAN	HOW OUT	BOWLER	RUNS	WKT	TOTAL	6s	4s	BALLS	NOTES ON DISMISSAL TOSS: ENGLAND.
11·03	11·31	636	1	S. WETTIMUNY	C⁺ DOWNTON	ALLOTT	190	5	442	·	21	471	RECORD SRI LANKA SCORE. Edged cover-drive off back foot. HIGHEST SCORE & ONE ABROAD
11·03	11·19	16	2	S.A.R. SILVA ‡	LBW	BOTHAM	8	1	17	·	1	11	Drove across full-length inswinger (left-handed batsman).
11·21	11·56	35	3	R.S. MADUGALLE	BOWLED	ELLISON	5	2	43	·	1	24	Off stump - played outside inswinger.
11·58	3·07	152	4	R.L. DIAS	C⁺ LAMB	POCOCK	32	3	144	·	3	104	Beaten by flight - low catch at mid-wicket.
3·09	2·19	248	5	A. RANATUNGA	BOWLED	AGNEW	84	4	292	1⁺	8	183	‡ 2+4 overthrows Beaten by breakback - off bail removed.
2·21	11·52	197	6	L.R.D. MENDIS*	C⁺ FOWLER	POCOCK	111	6	456	3	11	143	‡ BY 4 SRI LANKA CAPTAIN. HS in TESTS. Drove to mid-wicket boundary.
11·33	12·02	29	7	P.A. DE SILVA	C⁺ DOWNTON	AGNEW	16	7	464	·	3	27	TEST DEBUT. Edged leg glance to keeper. Well-judged catch.
11·54	(12·28)	34	8	A.L.F. DE MEL	NOT OUT		20			1	3	25	
12·04	(12·28)	24	9	J.R. RATNAYEKE	NOT OUT		5			·	·	18	
			10	D.S. DE SILVA	} DID NOT BAT								
			11	V.B. JOHN									

* CAPTAIN   ‡ WICKET-KEEPER   **EXTRAS** b 2 lb 8 w 2 nb 8   **20**

5⁺ 51⁺ 1006 balls (including 10 no balls)

TOTAL (166 OVERS, 692 MINUTES) **491 - 7 DECLARED**

14 OVERS 2 BALLS/HOUR
2·96 RUNS/OVER
49 RUNS/100 BALLS

BOWLER	O	M	R	W	NW	HRS	OVERS	RUNS
AGNEW	32	3	123	2	10	1	14	43
BOTHAM	29	6	114	1	-/1	2	14	38
ELLISON	28	6	67	1	7/1	3	14	42
POCOCK	41	17	75	2	-	4	17	50
ALLOTT	36	7	89	1	-	5	14	30
					2D	6	15	43
	166	39	491	7		7	15	25
						8	13	37
						9	14	62
						10	14	55
						11	15	31

2ⁿᵈ NEW BALL taken at 11·17 am on 2nd day –
SRI LANKA 229-3 after 85 overs

RUNS	MINS	OVERS	LAST 50 (in mins)
50	79	18·3	79
100	149	34·3	70
150	215	52·0	66
200	295	72·3	80
250	365	89·5	70
300	468	113·3	103
350	520	125·0	52
400	573	137·2	53
450	652	167·1	79

LUNCH: 81-2   28 OVERS   WETTIMUNY 54⁺
121 MINUTES   DIAS 7⁺ (66')

TEA: 173-3   59 OVERS   WETTIMUNY 108⁺
240 MINUTES   RANATUNGA 54⁺ (36')

STUMPS: 226-3   81 OVERS   WETTIMUNY 115⁺
BAD LIGHT at 5·38 pm – 25 min lost   330 MINUTES   RANATUNGA 54⁺ (66')

LUNCH: 271-3   103 OVERS   WETTIMUNY 137⁺ (4m)
RAIN at 12·00 pm (32 min lost)   419 MINUTES   RANATUNGA 74⁺ (3m)

TEA: 370-4   130 OVERS   WETTIMUNY 173⁺ (8m)
541 MINUTES   MENDIS 52⁺ (8m)

STUMPS: 434-4   144·5 OVERS   WETTIMUNY 187⁺ (6m)
RAIN 4·12-5·18 (96 min lost)   605 MINUTES   MENDIS 100⁺ (6m)

WKT	PARTNERSHIP		RUNS	MINS
1st	Wettimuny	Silva	17	16
2nd	Wettimuny	Madugalle	26	35
3rd	Wettimuny	Dias	101	152
4th	Wettimuny	Ranatunga	148	248
5th	Wettimuny	Mendis	150	176
6th	Mendis	De Silva	14	19
7th	De Silva	De Mel	8	8
8th	De Mel	Ratnayeke	27*	24
			491	

‡ SRI LANKA 4th WICKET RECORD.

compiled by BILL FRINDALL

ENGLAND 1st INNINGS   IN REPLY TO SRI LANKA'S 491-7 DECLARED

IN	OUT	MINS	No.	BATSMAN	HOW OUT	BOWLER	RUNS	WKT	TOTAL	6s	4s	BALLS	NOTES ON DISMISSAL
12·40	2·10	50	1	G. FOWLER	C⁺ MADUGALLE	JOHN	25	1	49	·	4	41	Steered short ball to 2nd slip - two-handed, chest-high catch
12·40	12·21	339	2	B.C. BROAD	C⁺ SILVA	DE MEL	86	3	190	·	8	242	HS in TESTS. Edged cut at short offside ball.
2·12	4·48	136	3	C.J. TAVARÉ	C⁺ RANATUNGA	DS DE SILVA	14	2	105	·	1	95	Mistimed pull-drive - mid-on catch.
4·50	1·46	194	4	D.I. GOWER*	C⁺ SILVA	DE MEL	55	4	210	·	5	151	Edged ball that 'left' him up slope.
12·24	5·50	267	5	A.J. LAMB	C⁺ DIAS	JOHN	107	9	369	1	10	195	4th in Tests this season. Pulled short ball to mid-wicket.
1·48	1·54	6	6	I.T. BOTHAM	C⁺ SUB (VONHAGT)	JOHN	6	5	218	·	1	6	Pushed across line - edged to gully.
1·56	4·09	114	7	R.M. ELLISON	C⁺ RATNAYEKE	DS DE SILVA	41	6	305	·	7	79	Mistimed pull - skier to extra-cover.
4·11	5·16	65	8	P.R. DOWNTON‡	C⁺ DIAS	DE MEL	10	7	354	·	1	53	Mowed simple catch to mid-wicket.
5·18	5·19	6	9	P.J.W. ALLOTT	BOWLED	DE MEL	0	8	354	·	·	1	Off stump out - 1st ball.
5·21	5·59	38	10	P.I. POCOCK	C⁺ SILVA	JOHN	2	10	370	·	·	21	First Test runs since 1976. Edged drive low to keeper's right.
5·52	(5·59)	7	11	J.P. AGNEW	NOT OUT		1			·	·	8	

* CAPTAIN   ‡ WICKET-KEEPER   **EXTRAS** b 5 lb 7 w 5 nb 6   **23**

1⁺ 37⁺ 892 balls (including 9 no balls)

TOTAL (147·1 OVERS, 618 MINUTES) **370** all out at 5·59pm on fourth day.

14 OVERS 2 BALLS/HOUR
2·51 RUNS/OVER
41 RUNS/100 BALLS

BOWLER	O	M	R	W	NW	HRS	OVERS	RUNS
DE MEL	37	10	110	4	3/1	1	13	53
JOHN	39·1	12	98	4	4/1	2	14	22
RATNAYEKE	22	5	50	0	-/2	3	15	23
D.S. DE SILVA	45	16	85	2	-/1	4	13	32
RANATUNGA	1	1	0	0	-	5	16	28
MADUGALLE	3	0	4	0	·	6	15	39
			23			7	13	45
	147·1	44	370	10		8	14	38
						9	17	39
						10	13	42

RUNS	MINS	OVERS	LAST 50 (in mins)
50	53	12·2	53
100	183	42·4	130
150	277	65·3	94
200	364	87·1	87
250	424	100·1	60
300	500	118·4	76
350	569	136·1	69

LUNCH: 32-0   5 OVERS   FOWLER 15⁺
21 MINUTES   BROAD 17⁺

TEA: 81-1   32 OVERS   BROAD 36⁺ (141')
141 MINUTES   TAVARE 12⁺ (89')

STUMPS: 139-2   61 OVERS   BROAD 69⁺ (259')
259 MINUTES   GOWER 16⁺ (70')

LUNCH: 210-3   91 OVERS   GOWER 55⁺ (198')
378 MINUTES   LAMB 16⁺ (84')

TEA: 300-5   119 OVERS   LAMB 55⁺ (159')
501 MINUTES   ELLISON 37⁺ (107')

SRI LANKA'S LEAD: 121 RUNS

WKT	PARTNERSHIP		RUNS	MINS
1st	Fowler	Broad	49	50
2nd	Broad	Tavaré	56	136
3rd	Broad	Gower	85	150
4th	Gower	Lamb	20	41
5th	Lamb	Botham	8	6
6th	Lamb	Ellison	87	114
7th	Lamb	Downton	49	65
8th	Lamb	Allott	0	1
9th	Lamb	Pocock	15	29
10th	Pocock	Agnew	1	7
			370	

compiled by BILL FRINDALL

SRI LANKA 2ND INNINGS (121 RUNS AHEAD ON FIRST INNINGS)

IN	OUT	MINS	No.	BATSMAN	HOW OUT	BOWLER	RUNS	WKT	TOTAL	6s	4s	BALLS	NOTES ON DISMISSAL
11·02	11·23	21	1	S. WETTIMUNY	C⁺ GOWER	BOTHAM	13	1	19	·	2	21	Edged late outswinger to 3rd slip.
11·02	(5·20)	316	2	S.A.R. SILVA †	NOT OUT		102			·	12	255	HS in Tests. Runner from 83". Maiden first-class hundred.
11·24	11·32	8	3	R.S. MADUGALLE	BOWLED	BOTHAM	3	2	27	·	·	9	Beaten by breakback that clipped off stump.
11·34	2·06	112	4	R.L. DIAS	LBW	BOTHAM	38	3	111	·	5	79	Beaten by breakback that kept low - played back.
2·09	2·15	6	5	A. RANATUNGA	LBW	BOTHAM	0	4	115	·	·	6	Late on quicker ball that 'straightened'. Hit on back leg.
2·17	2·21	4	6	P.A. DE SILVA	C⁺ DOWNTON	POCOCK	3	5	118	·	·	6	Edged 'arm' ball to 'keeper.
2·24	4·46	120	7	L.R.D. MENDIS*	C⁺ FOWLER	BOTHAM	94	6	256	3	9	96	Edged pull - skier to extra-cover.
4·48	4·59	11	8	A.L.F. DE MEL	C⁺ ELLISON	BOTHAM	14	7	276	·	3	8	Drove to deep mid-off.
5·02	(5·20)	18	9	J.R. RATNAYEKE	NOT OUT		7			·	1	15	
			10	D.S. DE SILVA	⎰ Did not bat								
			11	V.B. JOHN									

*CAPTAIN   †WICKET-KEEPER

EXTRAS   b 5   lb 4   w -   nb 11   **20**   3⁶ 32⁴   495 balls (including 15 no balls)

TOTAL (80 OVERS, 316 MINUTES)   **294-7** DECLARED at 5·20 pm on 5th day.

15 OVERS 1 BALLS/HOUR
3·68 RUNS/OVER
59 RUNS/100 BALLS

BOWLER	O	M	R	W	nb		HRS	OVERS	RUNS		RUNS	MINS	OVERS	LAST 50 (in mins)
AGNEW	11	3	54	0	15	1	11	48		50	60	11·3	60	
ALLOTT	1	0	2	0	·	2	16	45		100	124	28·4	64	
BOTHAM	27	6	90	6	·	3	17	42		150	213	51·2	89	
POCOCK	29	10	78	1	·	4	14	45		200	252	61·4	39	
ELLISON	7	0	36	0	·	5	16	98		250	280	68·4	28	
LAMB	1	0	6	0	·									
TAVARÉ	3	3	0	0	·									
FOWLER	1	0	8	0	·									

20
80   22   294   7
2nd NEW BALL not taken

LUNCH: 93-2 [27 OVERS / 119 MINUTES] SILVA 39* (115') DIAS 27* (87')
(214 AHEAD)

TEA: 180-5 [58 OVERS / 239 MINUTES] SILVA 71* (239') MENDIS 37* (77')

MATCH DRAWN

MAN OF THE MATCH: S. WETTIMUNY

(Adjudicator: T.W. Graveney)

TOTAL TIME LOST: 1 HOUR 55 MIN (NET)

WKT	PARTNERSHIP		RUNS	MINS
1st	Wettimuny	Silva	19	21
2nd	Silva	Madugalle	8	8
3rd	Silva	Dias	84	112
4th	Silva	Ranatunga	4	6
5th	Silva	PA De Silva	3	4
6th	Silva	Mendis	138	120
7th	Silva	De Mel	20	11
8th	Silva	Ratnayeke	18	18
			294	

Compiled by BILL FRINDALL

1985 – AN AUSTRALIAN YEAR

AUSTRALIANS REMEMBERED
Trevor Bailey & Fred Trueman

TREVOR BAILEY: 1985 sees the arrival of the Australian cricket team to tour this country. Like all their predecessors, their main objective will be to retain those mythical Ashes. Everybody, but particularly County Treasurers, will be hoping for another series like the Botham bonanza of 1981, which caught the imagination of the entire nation, not just cricket lovers, and demonstrated that there is something very special about an Anglo-Australian confrontation.

FRED TRUEMAN: I have always been excited by Tests against Australia and during our respective first-class careers, covering more than two decades, they have provided the highlights of international cricket. There were short periods when the West Indies and South Africa could claim to have the strongest team in the world, but for most of our era the unofficial crown was held by either Australia or England. Unfortunately, for the past decade the West Indies have been so powerful that it will be some time before a fight for the Ashes can once again claim to be also for the world championship.

TREVOR BAILEY: The greatest Australian batsman I ever bowled against was unquestionably Sir Donald Bradman. On all three occasions he scored a century, but I did have the honour of trapping him with a long hop after

he had decided to give it away for 143 in a festival match. It was generally agreed that in 1948 the Don was well past his peak and I am merely thankful I never had to bowl at him in his prime.

Who do you consider to have been the best Australian batsman you bowled at, Fred?

FRED TRUEMAN: You may be surprised by this, Trevor, but on the occasions I played against Australia, taking into account the runs he scored, the manner he made them in and the number of occasions he rescued his side, I think I must go for Peter Burge. Neil Harvey was a greater player, but I found bowling against Peter was usually more difficult.

TREVOR BAILEY: Although Australia has produced very many great stroke-makers in addition to Bradman, Harvey and Burge, they have always appreciated the value of a solid, dependable opening batsman, who can be relied upon to take on the role of sheet anchor. Before the war Bill Woodfull filled this role to perfection. Whose wicket did you most want to pick up early with the new ball?

FRED TRUEMAN: It has to be Bill Lawry by a very long way. Bill was a fine opener, who accumulated safely and steadily, pushing here and nudging there. If you sat and talked to Bill, he would say that in a Test Match his objective was to make around 40 runs per session, which would give him 100 or so at close of play. It would also provide his side, who would expect to go on batting until about tea time on the second day, with a solid base.

TREVOR BAILEY: Did you find there were certain batsmen you found it particularly frustrating to bowl against? Although by no means a great player, I personally detested having to bowl at Charlie Harris, because if he happened to be in a particularly obstinate mood, there seemed no way to remove him, short of dynamite. Is there an Australian player who falls into that category?

FRED TRUEMAN: I do not think I have ever encountered a more infuriating batsman than 'Slasher' Mackay. I reckon he knew where his off-stump was to within a quarter of an inch, which enabled him to leave alone balls which you yourself were convinced would bowl him. He was an outstanding player of quick bowling, but not so impressive against spin on a turning wicket.

TREVOR BAILEY: It has always been my contention that if 'Slasher' had played against us in Australia, when Frank Tyson caused so much havoc, we might not have won the Ashes; while it has seemed to me that a perfect purgatory for a cricket-lover like Jim Swanton would be watching me bowling against 'Slasher' in a timeless Test, or vice versa.

Since the war Australia have had a great knack of producing high quality pace bowlers, who have proved to be, especially in England,

The immortal Sir Don Bradman.

far more formidable than expected. Here are just a few instances of Australian bowlers emerging from obscurity to make a sudden impact at international level.

Many Australians thought the choice of Terry Alderman to tour England in 1981 was a mistake and nobody could seriously have thought that he would capture 42 wickets in the six Tests. Australia were not given too much hope when they toured England in 1972, but Bob Massie, an unknown, provided Dennis Lillee with ideal support, while at Lord's he gobbled up 16 wickets with one of the most amazing spells of swerve-bowling ever. More than a decade earlier Graham McKenzie, as a 20-year-old, captured 5 wickets at Lord's to mark the arrival of another outstanding Australian paceman in Test cricket.

Now, Fred, you and I have seen, over the years, all the most outstanding Australian pacemen since the war, but who was the best?

FRED TRUEMAN: For my money, nobody was in the same class as Ray Lindwall. What was so special about Ray? The late Wally Grout really summed it up when he said, 'He's a fast bowler of the highest class with the movement and the accuracy more associated with an outstanding medium-pace bowler'.

Ray had the most rhythmical run-up I have encountered. As a result he was so perfectly balanced when he entered his delivery stride that he was in complete control when he released the ball, which enabled him to avoid the little upsets, which trouble normal bowlers, such as long hops, half-volleys, no-balls, or, perish the thought, wides.

In addition to a beautiful action and a pace which by itself was sufficient to unsettle the class batsman and terrify the timid, he possessed three additional attributes. First, he had the heart and the stamina which enabled him to come back at the end of a long hot day to achieve that vital breakthrough. Secondly, he was a natural athlete, who would, and indeed did, excel at other sports. Finally, he had that killer streak which enabled him to find that extra venom when it was really necessary.

Ray was my one and only fast bowling idol and as a result I have often been asked if I modelled my own bowling on him, as there certainly were a number of similarities. However, there is no truth in that suggestion, because I had never seen him bowl until I played against him. On the other hand, if I had seen him when I was a kid, I am quite sure that I would have said, 'That's the way I want to bowl'.

Like anybody of my generation, whenever I think of Ray Lindwall, Keith Miller immediately comes to mind because they went together as naturally as ham and eggs, roast beef and Yorkshire pud or gin and tonic. They were the ideal pair of fast bowlers, because they complemented each other as, though both were performers of the highest quality, they were entirely different in approach, character and technique.

In addition to being a great fast bowler, Keith was not only the finest Australian all-rounder I have seen, but he was also a great entertainer, because there was more than a touch of genius about his batting, bowling and fielding.

TREVOR BAILEY: I always thought that Ray Lindwall was the most devastating new ball bowler I faced, because he had the ability to swing the ball at real pace more than anybody else. His natural swerve was away from the bat, which in the right conditions he could start on, and even outside the leg-stump, but he also mastered the in-swinger as a result of a year spent in the Lancashire League. It was with one of them he bowled me 'through the gate' to end my international career with a pair.

What especially impressed me about Ray was his control. Without any discernible change in his approach and rather round-arm action, Ray could send down a deadly yorker, perfectly camouflaged slower ball, or a bouncer which tended to skid through. However, with an old ball on a perfect pitch and the batsmen well set, I thought that Keith, providing he was in the mood, posed a greater threat as with his very high action he was liable to make the odd ball lift off a length, or deviate sharply off the seam.

Of the many other Australian pacemen with whom you played who stands out?

FRED TRUEMAN: Alan Davidson was easily the most accomplished left-arm opening bowler. From a brief, easy approach, he went into an ideal sideways-on body action which enabled him to swing the ball into the right-hand batsman from outside his off-stump and also sometimes to make the ball leave him off the seam.

When I saw 'Garth' McKenzie make his international debut at Lord's in 1961, I had the satisfaction of bowling him out on his twenty-first birthday and wishing him many happy returns. It was immediately obvious that he was destined to become one of their finest fast bowlers. In our second innings he took 5 for 37 in 29 overs which played a very big part in Australia's victory. One of the secrets of his success was that he was a little faster than his lively, economical run-up suggested and he was able to make the ball lift sharply from only just short of a length, even on a placid pitch.

Although I never played against him, I must mention Dennis Lillee, whom I always think of as the last of what I call the classic fast bowlers. From the moment I first saw him I admired his style. His run-up, action and follow through were all copy-book. That was why, when he had lost some of his original pace, he was still able to take wickets at the highest level.

Fast bowlers have always been more effective when they have been able to hunt in pairs and so I cannot talk about Dennis Lillee without saying something about 'Thommo', who came from nowhere to partner him against England in 1974–75. 'Thommo' with his slinging action and great speed was in fact the chief destroyer and 'hit-man' taking 33 wickets for less than 18 apiece.

TREVOR BAILEY: The main reasons for Australian success since the war have been the power and penetration of their pace attacks, supported by top-class fielding, especially the catching, and backed up by some fine batsmen. Their big weakness, which has applied more in England than in Australia, has been their slow bowlers. The majority have made little impact and captured relatively few wickets. I am still mystified as to why they have continued to send left-hand spinners to England despite the number of complete failures.

In Australia their slow bowlers have been more formidable, though I would estimate that the seamers have accounted for 80 per cent of the wickets. To me the most fascinating and the most difficult spinner was Jack Iverson, a freak leg-break and googly bowler with a unique grip. I never 'picked him' and played him, with complete lack of success, as an off-spinner. He was a very fine bowler; indeed he had to be, because he was easily the worst bat and fielder I have ever seen in an Australian Test team.

Who was the best Australian spinner you encountered?

FRED TRUEMAN: You are certainly right about the failure of their spinners in England, even Richie, who was, in my opinion, their best slow bowler, only took 23 wickets in three tours, but in Australia he was a very different proposition, largely because he was able to make the ball bounce. On one occasion Colin Cowdrey 'shouldered arms' against him only for the ball to bounce high enough to take a glove.

Richie was remarkably accurate for a wrist-spinner and was also the most astute of Australian captains, because he had flair, total command on the field and really knew the game, which he had studied very carefully. He was not afraid to put his theories into practice, and they often worked.

TREVOR BAILEY: I certainly agree that Richie was an outstanding skipper, though my pride of place goes to the Don, but Richie was unquestionably the finest captain in terms of public relations with the media. His Press interviews were models and I only wish some England skippers could acquire just a fraction of his skill in this area. The only complaint I ever heard about a Benaud interview with the Press was that he wanted to write the copy as well, and he probably would have done that rather better anyway!

Which of the Australian grounds did you prefer?

FRED TRUEMAN: Quite apart from it being the most beautiful, I always liked bowling at Adelaide, because it seamed about a little and I usually picked up some wickets there.

TREVOR BAILEY: That surprises me Fred, because I always found the Adelaide pitch very plumb and much preferred bowling at Melbourne or Sydney.

FRED TRUEMAN: Everybody used to say to me, 'Oh wait till we get to Sydney. You'll love it there, because it is green and you will be able to move the ball all over the place'. However, when I got there the pitch was just a brown strip, looking like a desert in the middle of an oasis.

On one occasion I flew up with my captain, Ted Dexter, from Tasmania to have a look at the Sydney pitch. We had won the Melbourne Test and wanted to get it absolutely right for the next one at Sydney. It was brown and bare and Ted asked me what I thought.

I said: 'It's obvious. We'll have to leave out at least one, possibly two, of our three fast bowlers, Statham, Caldwell and myself, who played a major part in the last Test'. This would have meant that we could play two spinners, David Allen and Ray Illingworth, in addition to Fred Titmus, and Ted could take the new ball, because the pitch was going to take spin from the outset.

When the rest of the party arrived, I remember Fred Titmus coming into the dressing-room a day before the match and telling David and Ray to get some Friar's Balsam on their fingers and go into the nets for some practice. He had seen the wicket and knew that it was likely to turn square.

Unfortunately, the opinion of two amateurs, David Sheppard, who had been out of first-class cricket for a long time (and should never have been selected), and Colin Cowdrey, carried more weight than that of the professionals who had to bowl on the pitch. As a result all three pace bowlers were included in the team and only one slow bowler, Titmus. He took 7 wickets for 79 runs in 37 overs, and we lost by 8 wickets, a game we would have won comfortably if we had picked our spinners. Quite apart from the wicket favouring spin, Australian batsmen did not play off-break bowling well.

Worse was still to come, because when we arrived at Adelaide, where the ball did seam about, we left out our third seamer and included a second spinner and drew a game we might well have won. Instead of winning the series 2–0, or possibly 3–0, we ended up all square because we had failed to capitalise on the conditions by not picking the right attack.

TREVOR BAILEY: Mistakes like that and odd selections do happen from time to time on tour. I remember Arthur McIntyre being chosen for the First Test at Brisbane as a batsman and emergency bowler on the evidence of his bowling in the nets.

Now what about Australian fieldsmen, Fred?

FRED TRUEMAN: In the outfield, or covers, two deserve all the superlatives, because they were magnificent, Neil Harvey and Norman O'Neill. Neil was exceptionally quick, neat with a very safe pair of hands and a deadly throw. You never took a quick single to him and later he became a brilliant slip. Norman not only stopped many shots which no normal fielder would even have considered stoppable, but he was a wonderful chaser of what others would have given up for boundaries. His throwing was fantastic, low, flat and just over the top of the stumps all the time.

Two also stand out in the close catching positions. I do not believe that there has ever been a better first slip to all types of bowling, slow and fast, than Bobby Simpson, and remember we had Phil Sharpe in Yorkshire, while Alan Davidson, 'The Claw', was a superb short-leg.

TREVOR BAILEY: I go along entirely with your quartet of fieldsmen, but think our choice of 'keeper will be different because I saw so much more of Don

Tallon, which makes me go for Don as the best Australian 'keeper because he was not just brilliant, he also possessed grace and style.

FRED TRUEMAN: You are right Trevor, mine must be Wally Grout. He may not have been too elegant, but he certainly held on to an incredible number of chances, as well as those half down the leg-side, which is what really matters. I also remember Wally catching me off Benaud at Adelaide for 0 in the first innings and again without scoring in the second, but this time Davidson was the bowler. In fact, I can remember all the many Tests I played against Australia. There is something different about those Australia v England ones which no other international, even an exciting one against the West Indies, ever produces.

TREVOR BAILEY: I am afraid I cannot recall the scores, individual or team, and players in all the Tests against Australia in which I took part, but numerous incidents remain with me. Like going to the cinema after the first day at Brisbane, having bowled out Australia for just over 200 on a beautiful batting pitch and hearing the rain beat down on the tin roof just before the final shoot-up between the outlaws and the sheriff. This meant that we had to bat on an Australian 'sticky'. It certainly proved an experience and produced 18 wickets, two declarations and a lovely sight (especially as I had two of them) of a score-board reading Australia 0 for 3 wickets!

I remember walking off the field at Old Trafford with Peter Richardson after Jim Laker had taken 19 wickets and commenting that we had seen the most remarkable bowling feat ever performed, and one which would never be equalled. The amazing feature was not so much that Jim should take 19 wickets, but that Tony Lock had only taken one on a pitch which started as a beach and turned into a genuine 'sticky'.

Savouring the irony of my having hit a 6 during a long vigil at Brisbane, which was worth £100, was sheer heaven. An Australian businessman had put up the money, its value over £1,000 today, for the first 6 hit in the Test. The opposition could not believe it, my own colleagues were surprised, but it did provide a memorable party by any standards.

The tension in our dressing-room at Adelaide. We only needed 92 runs to win the match and take the Ashes on a slow, easy batting pitch, and Lindwall was not playing! It looked a formality, but we had forgotten what Keith Miller could do. He bowled superbly and in 20 balls removed Hutton, Cowdrey and Edrich and we were eventually thankful to limp home with 5 wickets down.

Making the unintentional mistake of using my thumb instead of my bat to drop a Lindwall bouncer at my feet, I then discovered I could not hold

Don Tallon – Trevor Bailey's choice for Australia's best wicket-keeper.

the bat. An X-ray showed that my thumb was broken and coming out of the hospital I encountered one of those 'anything for a picture' photographers. I had been given an injection in the hope that it would enable me to continue batting and my thumb was plastered. His request for a picture of the injection hardly delighted me, as I am liable to faint at the sight of a needle. I explained it had already been done, but he said that was no problem. All he required was a nurse, a needle and my other hand and he would then reverse the negative!

What was your most memorable Test Match against Australia?

FRED TRUEMAN: There is absolutely no question, The Oval 1953, when we regained the Ashes, which had been held by the Australians since 1934. I was not only the youngest player in our side, but in those days it was a great honour to be selected against Australia, especially for a match which would decide the fate of the Ashes. It had been agreed to add an extra day in the event of no decision being reached in five days.

We beat what I have always thought a well above average Australian side and there was not much to choose between the two teams. Their seam attack was stronger than England's, they were slightly better in the field, and their batting had greater depth. We had Hutton and Compton, superior spinners, and Bedser. That is one match I shall never forget and shall always be grateful to have taken part in.

TREVOR BAILEY: And neither shall I, though I am a little vague about the evening. I seem to remember three night-clubs and dawn coming up as I was driven home.

ALAN McGILVRAY
Brian Johnston

One of the best bits of news in the summer was when Peter Baxter received a letter from Alan McGilvray. It confirmed that he hoped to come over here in 1985 to cover the six Australian Tests for what will be, for him personally, a Grand Farewell tour. We shall be delighted to have him with us in the box, and to help him celebrate his 100th commentary in Tests between England and Australia. 'McGillers' is an old friend of mine and this is what I had to say about him in my book *Chatterboxes* which Methuen published in 1983:

One or two older readers may remember someone called Jack Smith, the whispering baritone. He used to sing songs like 'Baby Face' and 'Miss Annabelle Lee' very softly at the piano during the Twenties and Thirties. For the past 50 years the Australian Alan McGilvray – from now on 'McGillers' – has been the whispering *commentator*. His style is utterly unique. He speaks right up against the microphone so confidentially and so quietly that even if you are sitting next to him, you cannot hear what he is saying. It is a very effective method as it gives the air of intimacy which makes the listener at home think that he is the one person to whom Alan is talking. His commentary flows freely at about the same level, his voice rarely generating excitement. His description of play is completely factual and he has always been wary of following the English style of 'colourful' commentary.

I would say he is the most unbiased commentator I have ever heard. He likes to enjoy good cricket, no matter who is winning, and has very high principles as to the conduct of players and the spirit in which the game is played. He is a fine reader of the tactics and cricketing skills and is well qualified to give his judgement. In addition to the experience gained during his 50 years of commentary, he also captained New South Wales in the Sheffield Shield in 1934–36. He succeeded Don Bradman as captain and had people like Bill O'Reilly and Jack Fingleton under his command, he himself being a useful fast-medium bowler.

One other unusual feature of his commentary is that he often looks through his binoculars while commentating, the field glasses resting on the top of the microphone, his elbows on the desk in front of him. I find this a very difficult thing to do, and BBC commentators rarely do it and then only for the odd ball or two. The trouble is that although you get a fine close-up of the batsman and the stumps, if the ball is hit anywhere, it goes out of your vision. It is then very difficult to take down the binoculars, and pick up where the ball has gone.

McGillers did his first cricket commentary in 1934, and so is by far and away the longest-serving and most experienced commentator. He broad-

BILL FRINDALL

Alan McGilvray, who makes his farewell tour of England in 1985.

cast his 200th Test at Melbourne in 1980, and received a tremendous ovation from the crowd when this fact was recorded on the giant score-board. He first came here to represent the Australian Broadcasting Commission in 1948 and has been here many times since. But his first Test broadcasts were done from an Australian studio when they were covering the 1934 and 1938 Test series in England with 'synthetic' commentary. McGillers and others would sit in front of a studio micro-phone and be fed with cables sent direct from England describing *each* ball, where it had gone, how many runs scored or how a wicket had fallen. There were certain code signs so that they were able to say, as the cable describing the second ball of an over was thrust in front of them,

'Bradman has cut that one down to third man – Leyland fields and returns over the top of the stumps to Les Ames, while they trot through for an easy single'. After some experience they could pick that up easily enough from the cable. But the difficult part was when the next cable was delayed for some reason, and to fill in they had to make up 'drinks coming out', 'a dog running across the pitch' and so on. It was all backed up by sound effects of applause, cheers or gasps for a missed catch or near thing.

I gather it all sounded very realistic and they were even still prepared to use the method in 1948, if the actual commentary being relayed from the grounds became too difficult to follow due to atmospheric interference. (In those days there was no Commonwealth cable laid to take the broadcasts.) It must, though, have been a tremendous strain on the commentators, having to improvise off the cuff, using only their knowledge of the game and their imagination. The first time this unusual system was used was in 1932 during Douglas Jardine's 'Bodyline' tour of Australia. A French radio station in Paris used Alan Fairfax who had played for Australia in England in 1930. He gave a ball-by-ball commentary from cables sent from Australia. He must have been exhausted at the end of the day, as there is no evidence that he had any assistant.

It must have all been good training for McGillers, who stands head and shoulders above any other Australian radio commentator. With the Sheffield Shield competition, and a regular visit each year from one of the cricketing countries, he gets plenty of practice. He has done a little television but basically has stuck faithfully to radio. I always remember a conversation he and I had with that great cricket enthusiast, Sir Robert Menzies. I have said that McGillers' commentary flows along more or less non-stop. So, I suppose, does mine. Anyway, Sir Robert told us that he enjoyed our commentaries but that he preferred so-and-so up in Brisbane, 'because he knows the value of the pause'. McGillers and I understood what he was getting at, but I'm afraid it did not have much effect on our style. Sir Robert was quite right. The commentator in question would say something like: 'He bowls.' Pause. 'Outside the off-stump.' Pause. 'The batsman plays and misses.' Pause. 'It goes through to the 'keeper.' He would then not say anything until the next ball was bowled, leaving a long gap as the bowler walked back to his mark. Imagine me keeping silent that long!

I had got to know McGillers well on his visits to Great Britain, but as I did television exclusively until the mid-Sixties, I had never worked with him until I went to Australia in 1958 for my three months' 'grace leave' with ABC. He was kindness itself in the box and a great help to me in my first attempts to give the score in the Australian way. We have since enjoyed 25 years of friendship in the commentary boxes of Australia, South Africa and England.

He has by now got used to our somewhat more light-hearted approach, with the jokes and the leg-pulls, and has been remarkably tolerant even when he has been a victim. I caught him beautifully two years ago at Lord's. Someone had kindly sent me a large and deliciously gooey chocolate cake for my birthday. I had cut it up into slices and was busy commentating when I heard McGillers enter the box behind me. I pointed at the cake, signalling that he should help himself to a slice. His eyes gleamed and I saw him take a large piece and pop it into his mouth.

As soon as the next ball had been bowled I immediately said, 'And now I'll ask Alan McGilvray what he thought of that last delivery'. There was a spluttering noise and an avalanche of crumbs as he desperately tried to speak with his mouth full. Ever since then he has never accepted even a biscuit or sweet in the box.

There was another occasion at Edgbaston in 1975 when he inadvertently reduced the box to complete silence for nearly 20 seconds, except for the sound of suppressed giggles. We were desperately trying to fill in time during a long period when a thunderstorm had stopped play. We were talking about the Chappell brothers and in particular the youngest one, Trevor. He had done the double in the Central Lancashire League the previous season, but we were not sure how much first-class cricket he had played for South Australia. 'Well,' I said, 'let's ask someone who should know the answer. He is sitting at the back of the box – Alan McGilvray. Alan, what about it?' I turned round and there indeed was Alan at the back of the box – but fast asleep. Everyone began to laugh and I had to make a quick decision. Should I let Alan down by saying that he was asleep, or should I pretend he had left the box? I chose the latter, although there was no real reason why he should not have been asleep – he was not on duty at the time. Anyway, I quickly said, 'I'm so sorry, but Alan must have just slipped out of the box. He was here a moment ago'.

Unfortunately Alan's subconscious mind heard his name and with a snort he suddenly woke up and said loudly, 'What's that? Does someone want me? What do you want to know?' By then that rotter Don Mosey had rushed from the box with his handkerchief stuffed into his mouth, and I was left alone with Trevor Bailey, who was having quiet hysterics to my right. It was too much for me and I began to laugh uncontrollably. There was no way in which I could speak. I covered up the microphone with my hand and for once there was complete silence from Test Match Special, except for some strange wheezing noises. After what seemed eternity but was in fact only about 20 seconds I apologised to the listeners and decided to come clean and explain what had happened. I must say Alan took it remarkably well but it took several minutes before we were able to return to normal.

McGillers is about five months younger than me, and will certainly be remembered – when he finally retires – as the longest-serving commentator, universally respected by his colleagues as the real professional, and with a large number of appreciative friends both in Australia and England. And I am sure that listeners everywhere would universally award him the supreme accolade of 'The man who *always* gave the score' – something I think we could all learn from him.